MARKERS ALONG THE WAY

**SMYTH & HELWYS**

Smyth & Helwys Publishing, Inc.
6316 Peake Road
Macon, Georgia 31210-3960
1-800-747-3016
©2020 by William Powell Tuck
All rights reserved.

*Library of Congress Cataloging-in-Publication Data*

Names: Tuck, William Powell, 1934- author.
Title: Markers along the way : the signs of Jesus in the Gospel of John /
by William Powell Tuck.
Description: Macon, GA : Smyth & Helwys Publishing, 2020. | Includes
bibliographical references.
Identifiers: LCCN 2020017542 (print) | LCCN 2020017543 (ebook) | ISBN
9781641732574 (paperback) | ISBN 9781641732581 (ebook)
Subjects: LCSH: Bible. John--Criticism, interpretation, etc. | Metaphor in
the Bible. | Signs and symbols--Religious aspects. | Jesus Christ.
Classification: LCC BS2615.52 .T83 2020  (print) | LCC BS2615.52  (ebook) |
DDC 226.5/06--dc23
LC record available at https://lccn.loc.gov/2020017542
LC ebook record available at https://lccn.loc.gov/2020017543

# Advance Praise for *Markers along the Way*

In recent years, as greater attention has been given to discover the historical Jesus, the Gospel of John has often been pushed aside in favor of the Synoptic Gospels. While John does offer a rather different portrait of Jesus, it is a mistake to ignore his portrayal of Jesus. In *Markers along the Way*, Bill Tuck brings the preacher's touch to John's focus not only on what Jesus does and says but on Jesus' identity. Directing his attention to ten signs he discerns in John's Gospel, we move from the miracle at Cana through the washing of feet, feeding of the 5000, and more, to the supreme sign, the resurrection, Tuck invites us to take hold of Jesus' true identity and let that transform our lives.

—Robert D. Cornwall
Pastor, Central Woodward Christian Church
(Disciples of Christ) of Troy, Michigan
Editor of *Sharing the Practice* (Academy of Parish Clergy)

While getting from one place to the next in life is not as much of a challenge as it once was, thanks to the numerous navigational aids that are now at our disposal, no such navigational aid exists for those who looking to locate the route to abundant life. Fortunately, Bill Tuck's explanation of the "markers" in the Gospel of John remind us that we are not at all helpless in that respect. His interpretations of each of them go well beyond a surface view of the Johannine signs, enabling us to understand better their implications for both then and now. Pastors will especially appreciate how Tuck's illustrations both enlighten Jesus' teachings and show how those who preach them might do the same for congregations today. All readers will benefit from a deeper recognition of how these markers point us to a stronger confession of Jesus as the Christ, the Son of the Living God, and how everyone who believes in him has life in his name.

—Doug Dortch
Senior Minister, Mountain Brook Baptist Church
Birmingham, Alabama

I have always loved the Gospel of John; it is full of elegant writing, and every story about Jesus seems to contain layer upon layer of meaning and significance. Ever the thoughtful and pastoral guide, Bill Tuck walks with us through John's Gospel, points out the signs of Jesus, and leads us to explore these layers of meaning—not only for Christ's journey of ministry, but also our journey of faithfulness to Christ. *Markers along the Way* is an insightful and engaging travel companion.

—Daniel E. Glaze
Pastor, River Road Church, Richmond, Virginia

Bill Tuck has done it again. He writes freshly, creatively, and relevantly. He is informed without being pedantic, eloquent without being cute, exegetical without being boring. I particularly like the balance of scholarship and "with it" present application. These studies could provide a platform for building a series of sermons or lessons. You must read about the thread that became a cable across Niagara. Take and read.

—Peter Rhea Jones
Professor Emeritus of New Testament
McAfee School of Theology, Mercer University

# William Powell Tuck

# Markers
## *along the* Way

### THE SIGNS OF JESUS
### IN THE GOSPEL OF JOHN

# Also by William Powell Tuck

*Facing Grief and Death*

*The Struggle for Meaning* (editor)

*Knowing God: Religious Knowledge in the Theology of John Baillie*

*Our Baptist Tradition*

*Ministry: An Ecumenical Challenge* (editor)

*Getting Past the Pain*

*A Glorious Vision*

*The Bible as Our Guide for Spiritual Growth* (editor)

*Authentic Evangelism*

*The Lord's Prayer Today*

*The Way for All Seasons*

*Through the Eyes of a Child*

*Christmas Is for the Young . . . Whatever Their Age*

*Love as a Way of Living*

*The Compelling Faces of Jesus*

*The Left Behind Fantasy*

*The Ten Commandments: Their Meaning Today*

*Facing Life's Ups and Downs*

*The Church in Today's World*

*The Church Under the Cross*

*Modern Shapers of Baptist Thought in America*

*The Journey to the Undiscovered Country: What's Beyond Death?*

*A Pastor Preaching: Toward a Theology of the Proclaimed Word*

*The Pulpit Ministry of the Pastors of River Road Church, Baptist*
(editor)

*The Last Words from the Cross*

*Lord, I Keep Getting a Busy Signal: Reaching for a Better Spiritual Connection*

*Overcoming Sermon Block: The Preacher's Workshop*

*A Revolutionary Gospel: Salvation in the Theology of Walter Rauschenbusch*

*Holidays, Holy Days, and Special Days*

*A Positive Word for Christian Lamenting: Funeral Homilies*

*The Forgotten Beatitude: Worshiping through Stewardship*

*Star Thrower: A Pastor's Handbook*

*A Pastoral Prophet: Sermons and Prayers of Wayne E. Oates* (editor)

*The Abiding Presence: Communion Meditations*

*Which Voice Will You Follow?*

*Beginning and Ending a Pastorate*

*The Difficult Sayings of Jesus*

*Conversations with My Grandchildren about God, Religion, and Life*

*To*
*Catherine and John*
*Who are special signs of God's love*
*Along life's way*

# Acknowledgments

I want to express a special word of appreciation to my former secretary, Carolyn Stice, who typed these pages during a busy and difficult time and who did it with thoroughness and supported all my efforts to finish them. Special thanks to Sandra Bundick, who helped me get the manuscript to its completion, and to Linda McNally, who carefully did the proofreading.

# Contents

# Preface

The Gospel of John is one of the most beautiful books in the Bible and one of the favorites of many Christians. It was written during a time of persecution to inspire Christians to stand firm in what they believed. The Gospel of John swells with a picture of an exalted Jesus who offers authentic life, which is not only realized in this world but reaches beyond the grave into eternal life.

Although the Gospel of John records none of the parables of Jesus, it contains several signs and wonders. "Their significance is primarily to point to Jesus' identity," Alan Culpepper writes, "though in John they also serve to show the fulfillment of expectations associated with Moses and the prophets (Elijah and Elisha)."[1] Usually there are seven signs denoted in John. But there are several other events that I think are clearly signs as well. The book also has numerous disclosures of Jesus, beginning with the phrase "I am." There are such phrases as "I am the light of the world," "I am the bread of life," and "I am the resurrection and the life."

All of these signs are presented by John as revelations about Jesus. They are in essence "parables" of the kingdom of God as seen in Jesus Christ. Rudolf Bultmann notes that the Evangelist does not focus on the power of the miracle worker "but [on] the divinity of Jesus as the Revealer."[2] These signs affirm that God's promises of the kingdom are realized in the life and work of Jesus. They are without question divine affirmations. John invites the reader to look to Jesus Christ to discover the One sent by God to bring salvation to the world.

Each of the signs presents an avenue into the nature of Jesus. Each sign reveals an aspect of his redemptive work. As we understand the meanings of these signs, we are drawn into a deeper awareness of God's love, grace, and redemption and of our own need for a deeper commitment to the One who has revealed to us what God is like. My prayer is that the reader will be drawn more closely to the self-giving God disclosed in Jesus Christ.

In an age deficient in humility and inflated with pride and arrogance, hopefully these signs from John's Gospel can remind us of Christ's invitation to respond to his call to discipleship. As we respond to Christ, we open our hearts and minds to welcome God into our lives. Instead of striving to be first, we humble ourselves to the God who comes to us through Jesus Christ.

## Notes

1. R. Alan Culpepper, *The Gospel and Letters of John*, Interpreting Biblical Texts (Nashville: Abingdon Press, 1998), 21.

2. Rudolf Bultmann, *The Gospel of John* (Philadelphia: Westminster Press, 1971), 119.

# Chapter 1

# The Sign of the New Wine

## *John 2:1-11*

The late English writer C. S. Lewis titled the story of his life and conversion experience *Surprised by Joy*. This title is descriptive of the great joy that Lewis "surprisingly" found in the Christian life. Why should he have been surprised to find joy at the center of the Christian faith? Unfortunately, many have equated the Christian life with solemn faces, somber personalities, doleful attitudes, and dull living. In the *Hymn to Proserpine*, Swinburne wrote of Jesus, "Thou hast conquered, O pale Galilean; the world has grown gray from Thy breath."

## The Signs of Jesus

Far from taking the color out of life, however, the New Testament resounds with the joy that was felt in the coming of Jesus. The angels proclaimed the "good tidings of great joy" that would be for "all people" (Luke 2:10). The writer of the Gospel of John declared that Jesus came into the world to make known the "abundant life" and that his joy might be established in the hearts of everyone (John 15:11).

In this study, we are beginning a pilgrimage in the Gospel of John by looking at what the author calls the "signs" of Jesus. The first sign, the changing of water into wine at Cana in Galilee, is a "frontispiece" by the Gospel writer to depict boldly the new joy that Jesus brought to the world. John selected seven miracles that he designated as "signs." Around these seven signs he revealed the nature and purpose of Jesus' life, death, and resurrection. The miracles are not presented as mere wonders but are signs that have deep spiritual meaning concerning the nature and mission of Jesus.

In the third chapter John shows Jesus cleansing the temple. This is not called a sign but is likely one. The other Gospel writers put the cleansing of the temple at the end of Jesus' ministry, but John is not concerned with chronology. He wants his readers to grasp the radical change that Jesus brought through his ministry. Jesus' miracles are "signs," parables, windows, or illustrations that point beyond the event of the moment to some deeper truth about Jesus.

The number seven is probably symbolic of the completeness that Jesus brings, but John states on several occasions that Jesus actually worked many more than seven miracles (John 2:23; 12:37; 20:30). By declaring that this wedding miracle was the first sign Jesus performed, John also ignores the legendary and apocryphal miracles about the childhood of Jesus that were circulating in his day. This, he emphatically states, is the first "sign." John wrote his Gospel around these seven signs so the reader could grasp quickly the extraordinary power and presence of the Christ he proclaims.

## A Festive Occasion

A wedding in ancient Palestine was a joyous and festive occasion. If a young woman was a virgin or had not been previously married, widowed, or divorced, the wedding ceremony would take place late at night. Rather than going away on a honeymoon, the couple spent a week at home entertaining their guests with an open house of feasting and rejoicing. The husband's family was responsible for making certain they had enough provisions for everybody who came. Often guests brought wine with them to assist the hosts.

John begins with the phrase "on the third day" (v. 1). But he doesn't tell us on the third day after what. Was it the third day after Jesus was baptized by John? Some scholars speculate that it may have been the third day after Jesus called Philip as his disciple. Others think it might be a reference to the resurrection of Jesus. If that were true, then the reference is even more symbolic in the author's mind.

## A Mother's Concern

Jesus arrived late to the celebration with his disciples. It was probably toward the latter part of the week, after much celebrating, that Mary, the mother of Jesus, indicated to her son that the supply of wine was almost depleted.

Her concern could indicate that she was in charge of the feast and may have been serving as a mother to a motherless bride, or she simply may have been assisting a relative. Some scholars have suggested that the bridegroom may have been one of Jesus' brothers, which might explain Mary's concern that everything go well. Some have also suggested that it might even have been John's wedding. Whatever the reason, her concern was evident since the wine supply was low. According to an old Jewish saying, "Without wine, there is no joy." Mary did not want to see the young bridal couple embarrassed by running out of wine. Mary had learned to depend on Jesus, her eldest son, since Joseph was probably dead by this time, and she instinctively turned to Jesus. She may also have been reminding him that he had arrived late to the party with his disciples and without any additional provisions; thus, he had caused the problem.

## The Son's Response

There is no way of knowing what Mary really expected Jesus to do when she told him, "They have no wine." Whether this was merely a suggestion to him or an attempt to force him to exercise his miraculous powers is not certain. The reply of Jesus sounds harsh and abrupt in our English translations, but in Greek it is really a respectful and tender one. The word "woman" denotes tenderness and courtesy. Jesus used it later on the cross to Mary—"Woman, behold your son" (John 19:26)—and in the resurrection garden—"Woman, why are you crying?" (John 20:15). "What have you to do with me?" also sounds harsh. The tone and the manner of Jesus' reply would have to be known before one could know for certain whether it was meant as a rebuke. With a twinkle in his eye, he may have said, "My dear, never mind; don't be worried. I'll take care of this in my own way."

On the other hand, Jesus may have been asserting his independence and indicating to his mother that everything he did, including any action regarding this embarrassing situation at Cana, must be in accord with his own sense of divine mission and purpose. "My hour has not yet come," he said (v. 4). Mary did not take her son's response as a rebuke because she immediately went to the servants and told them to do whatever Jesus asked them to do.

Six stone water pots, used for Jewish purification purposes, were standing in the vestibule of the banquet room. Water from the pots was used to wash the dust from the sandaled feet of guests as they entered the home. Water from these pots would also be used in the ceremonial hand-washing before the meal and, for the strict Jew, even between courses of the meal. If the wedding party were to be large, an abundant supply of water would be necessary. Each stone pot would hold about twenty-five gallons of water. Jesus told the servants to fill the pots with water, and they filled them to the brim. The fact that John indicates that the pots were filled "to the brim" (v. 7) is probably to suggest that there was no room for anything else to be added to them; no one would be able to explain away the miracle.

## When Our Provisions Are Inadequate

John says this is the first "sign" that Jesus did (v. 11). This sign is a difficult one for us to grasp today. Certain symbols leap out at me as I read this "sign." Maybe you share these with me. Who among us, like the family in this story, has not reached some point in life where we feel we have run out of wine? We have run out of provisions. Many of us have reached the point where we feel insufficient or inadequate. We all know the sinking feeling that comes when we realize that our supply cupboard is no longer full. It has run out. At this moment, we reach beyond our own resources to someone else who can give us the strength to go on.

Are there days in your life when you feel that you do not have the strength, power, or ability to keep going? To express it symbolically, you have run out of wine in your life. Then you reach out to someone else—to God. You look to God to sustain you and give you the strength to go on.

Jesus, then, instructed the servant to draw some out and take it to the master or headwaiter. Can you imagine the look Jesus got from the stewards when he told them to take this water in and serve it to the guests? They probably thought, "Who is this guy?" But Mary, who seemed to be in charge, instructed them to do whatever Jesus told them to do. And so they did. The steward of the feast, who was responsible for the service of the meal, tasted the wine before it was set before the guests and jokingly remarked, "Every man serves the good wine first; and then when men have drunk freely, then the poor wine; but you have kept the good wine until now" (v. 10). The steward's remark showed his surprise and pleasure that good wine was still available even at this late stage in the week's celebration. The feasting could go on!

## The First Sign

Are we to conclude from this account of the miracle at Cana that Jesus was primarily concerned about the quantity of wine that a young couple had at their wedding reception? Hardly! Pictorially and carefully, John has presented his episode and pointedly noted that this was the first of Jesus' signs. Jesus is presented here by John as much more than "the life of the party." Each of the seven signs is important, not just for its own sake but also for the deeper spiritual truth that each is seeking to unveil. Each sign points to a meaning beyond itself. For example, the feeding of the five thousand is a sign that Jesus is the "Bread of Life"; the healing of the blind man is a sign that Jesus is the "Light of the World"; and the raising of Lazarus is a sign that Jesus is the "Resurrection and the Life."

The miracle of changing water into wine is a sign of the inadequacy of Judaism and the offer to the world of joyous new life through the Son. The rest of John's Gospel can be described as a commentary on the symbolism in this sign. The Jews believed that seven was the perfect and complete number, while six, on the other hand, was seen as incomplete and imperfect. The six water pots, then, indicated the incompleteness and insufficiency of the Jewish religion. Water that was used ceremonially to clean a person externally had been transformed by the wine, which renewed internally.

## Jesus Brings New Life

Jesus himself is the wine of life who fulfills what Judaism had longed for. He makes complete their incomplete system. He is in reality what they anticipated. He is the one who is able to transform the water of the old law into the wine of the new covenant. If water is the symbol of the old way of Judaism, wine is the symbol of the gospel of Jesus. Wine becomes the symbol of the spiritual life and joy of the new covenant (Mark 14:24). The gospel of Jesus is the new wine that bursts the old bottles (Mark 2:22). The kingdom of God is depicted as a vineyard (Mark 12:1-9). Jesus himself is pictured as the "real vine" (John 15:1). In many places in the New Testament, the wedding image is used to show the relationship of Jesus to his disciples or to the church (Mark 2:19-22; John 3:29; Eph 5:31-32). One of the self-chosen titles, which Jesus often used to refer to himself and his relationship to his disciples and the church, was "Bridegroom" (Matt 9:14-15; Luke 5:33-35).

Judaism, as the water of purification, is fulfilled when Christ turns it into the wine of eternal life. This is the message of the miracle of Cana: Judaism was incomplete within itself and had to be transformed by the Son who brought new life, as symbolized by the new wine. It makes little difference whether one believes that all the water in the stone pots became wine or only what was drawn out by the servants. The chief emphasis is on the power of Jesus to transform the water into wine, the old into the new, staleness into freshness, despair into hope, and, ultimately, death into life.

The first sign denotes that whenever Jesus comes into a life, a transformation takes place that is like turning water into wine. Later, the action of Jesus in cleansing the temple when he turned over the moneychangers' tables revealed that he was bringing in his kingdom in a revolutionary way (John 2:15). His way would upset the customs and traditions of his people.

## A Sign of Divine Significance

The sign at Cana served as a means of revealing the glory or the divine significance of who Jesus was. The disciples "believed" (v. 11) not merely in the sense of believing what he said to be true but in the sense of committing themselves in personal trust. They believed that the Messianic age had dawned in Jesus. It is interesting to note that everyone at the feast did not believe. The head steward tasted the wine and said, "Oh, this is wonderful." He didn't say, "Isn't Jesus the Messiah?" Those who merely oohed and ahhed at the taste of the new wine did not recognize the Messiah. The headwaiter did not know where the wine came from, nor did most of the guests. The servants could only wonder.

The disciples sensed the sign in this miracle because they already had some measure of faith. This act for them marked the beginning of the new age that was to come. Gail R. O'Day observes,

> The extravagance of Jesus' act, the superabundance of the wine, suggests the unlimited gifts that Jesus makes available. The story invites the reader to share in the wonder of the miracle, to enter into the joyous celebration made possible by Jesus' gift. The story invites the reader to see what the disciples see, that in the abundance and graciousness of Jesus' gift, one catches a glimpse of the identity and character of God.[1]

The words "my hour has not yet come" were a reminder that Jesus' cup would ultimately be the one where his blood would be "poured out for many" in a sacrificial death (Mark 14:24). The disciples had not seen a complete manifestation of his glory but would continue growing in their understanding of who he was. Later they would be able to declare, as John does in his prologue, "We beheld his glory, the glory of the only begotten of the Father" (John 1:14).

## The Joy of the Christian Life

The disciples believed. They were able to see through this veiled image something of the manifestation of God's love and grace. The wine is symbolic of the joy that Jesus Christ can bring into your life and mine. When you and I commit our hearts and lives to Jesus Christ, as the early disciples did, he brings into our lives a new attitude, a new perspective, a new birth. He changes the water, the flatness of our lives, into the radiant, sparkling wine of God's presence. He forever makes our lives different. When I was working on this chapter, I turned to *The Handbook of Theology* to look up the word "joy" and discovered that it was not even in the book. Just think, the word "joy" was not in this theological dictionary! However, the word "joy" occurs as a noun in the New Testament fifty-eight times, and the verb "rejoice" occurs seventy-three times. Paul uses the phrase "rejoice in the Lord" fifteen times.

Wine is symbolic of the joy that Jesus Christ brings to our lives. When this joy is absent, we are conscious of how inadequate, incomplete, and unfulfilled we are without his presence. Christ gives us a new sense of hope, life, and inner joy. Paul Tillich, the late American theologian, once wrote,

> Joy is more than pleasure; and it is more than happiness. Happiness is a state of mind which lasts for a longer or shorter time and is dependent on many conditions, external and internal. . . . Happiness can stand a larger amount of pain and lack of pleasure. But happiness cannot stand the lack of joy.[2]

Joy is the expression of our essential and central fulfillment. Jesus Christ gives us this joy—an inner joy that cannot be taken away from us by the conditions around us. We are aware of God's sustaining spirit in our lives, and that makes all the difference.

This doesn't mean that we will always be grinning. There are indeed times when life is difficult. Christian joy is different from the world's happiness. It is a joy that gives us inner security. We know that the One who changed water into wine is present in our lives to sustain us, hold us up, bear us up, support us, comfort us in our grief, be with us in our sickness, and help us shoulder our burdens so we do not face them alone. We have experienced times when our own resources were insufficient. But through God's grace we found strength and power to go on. This joy has also enabled us to focus on the needs of others and not only on ourselves. As Archbishop Desmond Tutu reminds us, "ultimately our greatest joy is when we seek to do good for others."[3] We who are followers of Christ have experienced this inner joy, and we strive now to share it through service to others.

I heard about a man who earned his living as a cabinetmaker. Unfortunately, he had become an alcoholic and soon slipped into the pit of despondency. Many thought his situation was hopeless. Through the help of friends who worked with him for many months, his life was turned around. He became a Christian and slowly got control of his struggle with alcohol. Later, as he was talking with some of his former drinking friends, one of them teasingly asked, "Now, do you really believe that Jesus turned water into wine?" The man looked at his friend and responded, "I don't know. But I can tell you this. Jesus has turned beer into furniture in my home. He has changed me, and I can now work again."

Our purpose, as I believe was John's, is not so much to focus on the literalism of the story as to discover the sign that John was seeking to tell about Jesus Christ. Jesus is the new wine, the one who comes into our lives and gives us joy, stability, and hope. In him we see revealed the glory of God. He comes into your life and mine to turn staleness into freshness, despondency into trust, hopelessness into hope, and selfishness into service.

Arthur John Gossip was a great hurricane of a Scottish preacher. A woman who had lived for a long time in a dark cellar apartment came under the influence of his preaching. After several months she was converted. Then she moved. A friend asked her, "Why did you move?" "Nobody," she said, "can live in a cellar and listen to Arthur John Gossip preach."

When our lives have been touched by Jesus Christ, he moves us out of the dungeons of life and opens our eyes to the brightness, radiance, and joy of life all around us. He invites us to go on a pilgrimage with him to find the abundant life. As John will write later, "This is eternal life to know Jesus Christ" (17:3). Eternal life does not begin after we die; it begins in this life through a new relationship in Christ. Our lives are then filled with marvelous joy. This day, celebrate the joy that Jesus Christ gives you as Lord. He is the sign of new life, new beginning, new hope, and new possibilities. Let us rejoice and be glad.

## Notes

1. Gail R. O'Day, "The Gospel of John," *The New Interpreter's Bible* (Nashville: Abingdon Press, 1995), 540.

2. Paul Tillich, *The New Being* (New York: Charles Scribner's Sons, 1955), 149.

3. Dalai Lama and Desmond Tutu, *The Book of Joy* (New York: Penguin Random House, 2016), 59.

# Chapter 2

# The Sign of Faith and Life

## *John 4:46-54*

Late one evening the telephone rang. When I answered it, a woman said, "Pastor, this is Jean Cartright. I am at the hospital. Our daughter has had a cerebral hemorrhage. We need you." I immediately went to the hospital to be with the family. For ten days I walked with the family as their daughter struggled to live. She was kept alive on a life-support system. She was only sixteen years old. On the tenth day she died.

John records a story in his Gospel about another parent whose child was at the point of death. A man pleaded with Jesus to save his son's life. We do not know a great deal about this man. We are told that he was a nobleman—an official—attached in some way to the royal court. He was likely a Gentile. Some scholars feel that this story may be another version of the account of the centurion recorded in Matthew (8:5-13) and Luke (7:1-10). There are similarities but several differences. The official lived in the seacoast town of Capernaum, which was about twenty miles from Cana. He had heard about Jesus, so he made the journey from the lowlands up to the highlands to see if this physician could help. He had obviously tried the remedies and physicians at hand, but they had not been able to assist his son. This story is a study in faith.

## His Faith Arose Out of His Need

Notice that the officer's faith arose out of his own need. The word in Greek that is used for son is "my little child." He obviously loved his son. He was willing to swallow his pride, put aside his position of authority and power, and seek out an itinerant rabbi, a wandering preacher of whom people said, "He might be able to help your son." When he met Jesus, he did not say, "Look who I am. I am an important person, connected with the Roman government." He didn't say, "My child is a good son. He is an important person because he is a wealthy man's child." He simply approached Jesus with "hat in hand" and expressed his need. A cry arose within his soul and he voiced the hope that Jesus might help.

Take a moment and observe that without his son's illness, without the distress it caused, he would never have turned to Jesus. He would never have thought of seeking Jesus if he had not had a deep need. His need opened the door to grace. Sometimes the first moment that people really turn to God is in a time of distress, a time of need. Their need convinces them that their own resources are inadequate, and they turn to God. Some pray to God for the first time in a moment of distress.

## Look at Your Own Need

I don't know what your need is, but I know that every single person either has had or is going through or will go through a time of crisis. At those moments we realize that our own strength is not adequate and reach out for some power, some strength beyond our own. As I have talked with people in the hospital, in homes, or over the telephone, I have felt the pulse of human need. I have talked with an individual suffering from a brain tumor, people in different stages of cancer, a wife whose husband just had bypass surgery, a man who is recovering from surgery, another who has had heart trouble, others suffering from depression and loneliness, and still others struggling under their burden of grief. A daughter has just learned of her mother's death. Another daughter has received word that her father has cancer. There are burdens and needs all around us. Many of you bear a heavy load unknown to others. We have discovered that we need strength beyond ourselves to sustain us.

Several years ago, I visited a man in a hospital. He had cancer. "I no longer ask *why*," he said. "I ask *what*. What must I do now to bear this burden? What direction do I take with my life now?" For some, our need, like that of the man in our text from John, drives us to God. His need gave birth to faith.

## A Secondhand Faith

Look at the stages of the official's faith. John reveals that the father's faith was progressive as his understanding of who Jesus is slowly deepened. He began with a secondhand faith. We do not know where the father first received knowledge of Jesus. Someone may have told him about Jesus. He may have heard about Jesus' healing power as it was rumored around the courts. During one of his business trips, he may have first heard a word about Jesus circulating through a crowd. Maybe he had witnessed one of the wonders Jesus had done.

He began, like we all do, with a secondhand knowledge of Jesus. We first learn about Jesus from our parents, Sunday school teachers, ministers, friends, or others. They tell us about God and Christ. This secondhand knowledge opens the door so we can then meet the living Lord of life.

Years ago, Voltaire, the noted French agnostic, was walking down the street with a friend, and a religious procession passed by. As the crucifix passed in front of him, Voltaire lifted his hat. "What?" his friend asked. "Have you, too, found God?" "Ah," Voltaire said, "we salute, but we do not speak."

Too many only nod to God, without having a real sense of God's presence. A secondhand relationship with God is never enough. It is the beginning point. But hopefully this shallow faith can be a stepping-stone to help us move beyond our hearsay faith to a personal relationship with God. Our faith then will rest not merely on what others have told us but on our own experience with Jesus Christ as Lord.

# A Limited-perspective Faith

Next the official moved into what I would call a limited-perspective faith. He asked Jesus to come down to his town and lay his hand upon his son. He thought that the only way Jesus could do anything for his son was to come to his town and touch his son. Many of us have our own perspectives and ideas about the way God is supposed to work in our lives to meet our needs or guide us. Sometimes we attempt to confine or restrict God by our limited perspectives. But God is not going to be limited by our views. God may approach our lives to guide us and direct us in ways totally different from what we have ever expected. Too often we limit God by our own perspectives.

# Sensationalism Is Not Needed

At the next stage, we observe that Jesus rebuffed the father for his desire for signs and wonders. Jesus' response to the pleading of the father for help is, "You, too, want a sign? Does everybody have to have some sign or wonder to believe?" His response seemed cold, heartless, uncaring, and unsympathetic. Maybe Jesus was directing a warning to his listeners that they could not build an adequate faith on a concept of sensationalism or miracles. Jesus had departed from Judea for a while because these folks always wanted another sign, another miracle. "Your faith cannot be built on that kind of sensationalism," Jesus avowed. Jesus knew that people always have a difficult time determining when a sign is really a sign or when a sign is merely sensationalism.

One of my favorite cartoonists is Doug Marlette, who used to draw the Kudzu cartoon about the Reverend Will B. Dunn. Dunn is an old-fashioned-looking preacher who is almost always dressed in a black suit and a black Pilgrim-type hat. In one cartoon, Will B. Dunn has decided to run for president. He has been asking God to give him a sign on whether he should enter politics or not. As he is walking along one day, he sees a burning bush. A voice speaks out of the burning bush: "Pssst! . . . Preacher!" "Holy catfish!" Dunn responds. "A Burning Bush!" The voice from the bush speaks directly to him. "Will B. Dunn! Let this be a sign unto you. Get out of the presidential race! . . . You're in over your head! Go back to your pastoral duties! . . . Give up and get out right now! . . . Do you hear me? You have no business in politics! . . . so get out!" In the next scene you see the preacher with a fire extinguisher in his hand squirting it on the bush. "Sploosh" goes the sound as he puts out the flame on the bush. Dunn then walks away, looking at the readers and observing, "Remember—only you can prevent forest fires!"[1]

How do we react when God gives us a sign? When our religion is based on sensationalism, we continually look for burning bushes. But even when we see them, we do not perceive their message. To build your faith on the necessity of signs is to build it on a shaky foundation indeed. Jesus warned the father and the listening crowd that they needed a firmer foundation for an authentic faith than signs and wonders. Our faith must rest on deeper resources.

The rebuff of Jesus may have been a test to see if the father's pleas were genuine. Was he really in earnest about his request? The Carpenter must first challenge shallow faith. He had to test the depth of the father's conviction. The Comforter must first be convinced.

But listen. The father continues to pour out his heart. He seems to say, "Lord, this is not a time for a lesson in theology. This is not a time to test my faith. Lord, my son is dying. Come, help him." He continues to plead intently for Jesus to help him.

## Taking Jesus at His Word

The next stage of the man's faith is evidenced in his response when Jesus says, "Go home. Your son will live." Jesus refused his request to go home with him but gave him a much greater and quicker response than he had expected. The father took Jesus at his word. There is nothing in the story about the man saying, "Now wait a minute, Jesus. How do I know that is true? Give me some evidence that this miracle has happened. Give me some proof." There is no argument, no debate. The story says he simply took Jesus at his word.

This father did not react like Naaman, who went to the prophet Elisha to be healed of leprosy. When Elisha told Naaman to go bathe in the Jordan River, he was insulted and turned to leave. But his slave got his attention when he said, "Now, wait a minute, Master. If Elisha had asked you to do some great thing, you would have done it. But he asked you to do a very simple thing: 'Go and bathe in the Jordan.' Why don't you do what he commanded and see what will happen?" Naaman did, and he was healed. But he almost missed the cure because of his pride. (See 2 Kings 5.) Suppose this father in John 4 had said, "I am not going back until you give me some clear evidence." Would his son have been cured? It seems unlikely. But there was no argument. There was only acceptance. He took Jesus at his word. Jesus spoke and the man believed.

I am convinced that often you and I do not really understand or hear or feel or sense God's word to us because we are too busy debating the issue, too busy arguing our own point. We are too busy insisting on what we think is supposed to be God's way. Sometimes we are overcome by indecision. We can't decide whether we should or should not do something. Many of us continuously grapple with indecision.

## Christ's Presence Is Not Limited

Suppose you are on a boat floating down the Ohio River. You are trying to decide whether or not you want to get off at the port in Louisville, Kentucky. As you are approaching the dock, you still can't decide if you want to stop. All the time you are trying to decide, you keep floating. Soon, if you don't decide to dock, you will find yourself in the waterfall. What you need to remember is this: not deciding is to decide. Some of us cannot decide whether to take God at his word or not. Indecision is deciding; it is deciding to reject God. Jesus said, "He that is not for me is against me" (Matt 12:30; Luke 11:23).

The father in our text accepted the word of Jesus. What a marvelous message for the church. This man, who was a Gentile, received the healing power of Christ for his son by Jesus' word alone. This has been the message to the church through the ages. The power of Jesus is not limited to his physical presence. We have his word. People who are separated by time and place from the historical Jesus can be encouraged. Jesus is not confined to the past. He is present today through the power of his living word. We trust in Christ's word and do not rely on signs. We remember his words to Thomas: "Blessed are those who have not seen but believe" (John 20:29).

Christ has given us his word that he will be present in our lives, and we can lean on him for strength and guidance.

Scholars have debated for centuries why this official seemed to take so long to get home. He had made the long journey to see Jesus in one day. He was given the word by Jesus at one o'clock that his son would live. We are not sure exactly what time he left Cana. Did he have business that he had to do for the king or whomever he was serving? Did it take him a while to round up the rest of the people with whom he was traveling? Was his camel too tired to travel? Did he start back that afternoon and the weather got so bad that he had to stop? Was he just weary? We don't know, but for some reason he was delayed. The next day the nobleman was met on the road by one of his servants. His servant brought him good news: "Master, Master," he cried. "Your child is well." The official asked his servant what hour his child got well. He was told that it was one o'clock (v. 52). That was the very hour that Jesus told him, "Your son will live." The father's faith was affirmed by the message from the servant. Knowing when his son got well was corroborating proof to the father.

John was trying to tell his readers that they did not have to have the bodily presence of Jesus Christ to experience his available power. The church does not rely merely on the memory of Jesus in the first century but has the assurance of the availability of his presence through the "word" today. His word is adequate.

## He Shared His Faith

When the nobleman arrived home, we see evidence of the next stage of his faith. At home he shared his faith with others. Can you imagine this man's joy when he heard from his servant that his son was well? It was then that he told his family about how Jesus Christ had healed his son with a word. After arriving home, the official told his family about his experience with the prophet from Nazareth. John states that the man's whole household believed (v. 53). When a person has had an authentic experience with Jesus Christ that has been life changing, then they will want to share that experience with someone else.

# The Second Sign

John concludes by saying that this was the second sign Jesus did. Oh, John knew about other miracles. But this was the second sign at Cana. What was it a sign of? First, it was a sign of the man's faith. The stages of the progression of his faith were evident.

The resonance of faith within this nobleman was clear. He looked away from his own resources and toward God. Is this kind of response what Samuel Miller means when he describes faith as "resonance"? "There is a resonance between God and the world; they fulfill each other, God speaking through the world, and the world finding its answer in God."[2]

But this sign is also a paradox. It is a sign that we don't need signs. The message of this text focuses on a sign that tells us we should not depend on signs. We simply take Christ at his word.

The healing of the official's son was also a sign about life. A son who was ill did not die, but he lived. John began his Gospel by declaring about the Word that "In him is *life* and the *life* was the light of men" (John 1:4). When Jesus spoke to Nicodemus, he told him that everyone who believes will have eternal *life*. Jesus spoke to the woman at the well in Samaria and told her about the water of *life* that he had come to bring. This story with the father and his son is also about the One who brings life. Christ as the giver of life is one of John's main themes. Later the Apostle Paul wrote, "For me to live is Christ" (Phil 1:21). Paul felt that his life was forever changed when he met Jesus Christ on the Damascus Road. Augustine had his life changed forever when a voice said, "Take up and read." Martin Luther was never the same after he discovered the passage that "the just will live by faith." John Wesley's heart was strangely warmed in the Moravian church, and his life was forever changed.

All of these people and thousands of others have found the *life* Christ gives through *faith*. When Jesus Christ comes into your life, he gives you a new perspective, a new direction, and meaning for living. If you are a Christian, you can remember when Jesus Christ gave you a different perspective on life. This came through your forgiveness of sin and through the opportunity to begin anew. He gave you a new way of understanding other people, God, and yourself. Jesus has come that we might have life.

Several years ago, I read how a suspended bridge was built across the Niagara River before construction crews had our modern-day equipment. The crew began by flying a kite across the river with a thread attached to it. A worker was on the other side of the river and secured the thread. Then he pulled a piece of string tied to the thread across the river. Then they tied a piece of rope to the string and pulled the piece of rope across. Finally, they tied a piece of cable to the rope and pulled it across. Once the cable was secure, they began their work of building the bridge. The work began with a thread.

Your faith may begin in a small thread-like way. This nobleman's faith was imperfect, shallow, and inadequate. No person comes to God full grown. We are all in the process of developing and growing in our faith. But the good news of the gospel is this: no matter how small your faith is, God will respond to you. Everyone begins with a small faith. Hear the word of God this day. Remember that God wants to reach out and touch your very being and give you life. As you open your heart, let Jesus Christ come in. The life he will give you can make all the difference in the world in who and what you can be.

## Notes

1. Doug Marlette, *I Am Not A Televangelist!* (Atlanta, GA: Longstreet Press, 1988), 83.

2. Samuel H. Miller, *The Dilemma of Modern Belief* (New York: Harper & Row, 1963), 78.

# Chapter 3

# The Sign of the Example of Service

## *John 13:1-17*

Recently, a church member told me that one of the most vivid memories he had from his small rural church was the service of foot washing. I don't expect that too many of us have actually participated in church foot-washing services. Some church traditions observe foot washing as an annual practice of their Maundy Thursday liturgy. Monks in Benedictine monasteries wash the feet of guests as a part of their hospitality. But among many church groups today, especially Baptists, any talk about foot washing usually brings only snickers or sneers.

## The Ancient Roads

Reflect with me for a moment what the roads were like in ancient Israel two thousand years ago. They had no paved roads like we do today, of course. Their roads were dusty, and if it rained they were muddy. The roads were also littered by the droppings from sheep, oxen, donkeys, and other animals used for transportation or bearing goods. Dusty, dirty, and muddy roads were a part of everyday life. People did not wear shoes but sandals. It was the practice in every home to wash one's feet before entering a house after traveling on a dusty road. Sometimes each person washed his or her own feet. Sometimes the wife or small children had this responsibility. If a person were affluent enough to have slaves, a slave was assigned this task. Jewish law, however, excluded a Jewish slave from this servile chore.

## The Foot-washing Episode

John is the only Gospel writer to record the foot-washing episode. He seems to depict the setting of this story on the night before the Passover. The other Gospels set the Last Supper on the night of the Passover celebration itself. John, however, shows Jesus being crucified on the Passover. You can debate whose chronology is correct. John's purpose was to depict Jesus as the Paschal Lamb. Raymond Brown, the noted New Testament scholar, observes that there is nothing in the Passover tradition that can be compared to foot washing.[1] This episode, then, was simply an occurrence that arose out of the need at a particular moment.

## The Humility of Jesus

Let's see if we can capture something about the meaning of this story. We will begin by taking the traditional approach that sees this story primarily as a sign of the humility of Jesus. What prompted Jesus to initiate this acted parable? The attitude of the disciples as they approached this meal likely gives us a clue. Many scholars feel that the disciples were probably debating who was going to be the greatest in the kingdom of God right before they came to the table. The question about who was to be the greatest was the foremost topic on their minds that night. The air was thick with hostility. Angry thoughts were directed at the two disciples who thought they were going to be "big shots" in Jesus' kingdom when he came into power.

## A Duty No One Wanted

The disciples likely took turns with the duty of washing the feet of the other disciples. No one disciple would have had this task all the time. Whoever's turn it was this night ignored it. As the disciples came in for the Passover meal, they reclined on cushions or on the floor beside the table. Everything in this scene has overtones of a Passover meal, even if John does depict it as taking place on the night before the sacred meal. Because of the heated debate about who was going to be first, no one was going to stoop to do a slave's work of washing somebody else's dirty feet.

## The Desire to Be Number One

Before you blame the disciples from centuries ago, it seems to me that the problem still persists. Doesn't it? Whispers about who is the greatest are still with us. Listen to them: "Oh, they overlooked me. My name wasn't listed." "I'm not going to be in the choir anymore. They never ask me to sing a solo." "I'm going to quit the youth group. They didn't give me a speaking part in the youth-week program." "If I can't be chairman, I'll not be on the committee." "I'd like to recommend my son to you for your job. He is really fantastic." "I thought my son would be chosen captain of the football team." "Why wasn't my daughter chosen class president?"

We know these feelings; the desire for recognition, applause, acclaim, and accolades dominates our life. We want, like the disciples, to be number one. We want to be recognized. In poll after poll with young people and adults today, few people want jobs that call them to serve. Rather than serving others, most people want somebody else to do something for them. The paramount desire seems to be to make a lot of money!

## Jesus Took a Towel and Basin

John says, "Jesus took a towel and basin." The King James translation gives an incorrect image. Jesus did not wait for the meal to be over before he got up. Jesus got up and girded himself in the middle of the meal, as though he could stand it no longer. Did he wonder why no one had accepted the customary duty of washing the feet of the disciples? He could feel the tension among them, so he stopped eating and took a towel and basin. He might have taken a sword as a sign of religious power. He might have taken gold as a sign of monetary power. He might have taken the Torah as the sign of religious power. He might have taken a crown as a sign of political power. But he took a towel and basin—a sign of humility and service—and washed the feet of the disciples. "In Christ," observes Brian McLaren, "we see an image of God who is not armed with lightning bolts but with a basin and towel, who spewed not threats but good news for all, who rode not a war-horse but a donkey . . . ."[2]

## Inclusive Love

Why did Jesus perform this humble act of a servant? John tells us, "Because Jesus loved them to the limits" (13:1, my translation). He loves the disciples to the "uttermost." Jesus loved *all* of the disciples. Judas was not excluded. John clearly indicates that Jesus knew he was going to be betrayed by Judas. Jesus washed the feet of all the disciples, including Judas. Can you imagine Jesus tenderly washing Judas's feet? Up to the end Jesus tried to reach Judas. Did Jesus whisper to him, "You still have an opportunity to turn away from your act of betrayal"? Were there still some words of love that were projected? We do not know. But the only defense Jesus used was love. Even his touch, however, could not deter Judas.

## A Sign of Cleansing

Jesus washed the feet of the disciples, and this acted parable symbolized humility and service. But this action was much more than that. It was also a *sign of cleansing*. When Jesus approached Peter, the "big fisherman" was filled with astonishment and shame because he had been unwilling to perform the fatigue duty of washing the feet of the other disciples. "No, Lord," Peter exclaimed, "you can't wash my feet." It was an honor for a disciple to wash his rabbi's feet. But to have a rabbi wash a disciple's feet! Peter could not grasp that. "If I don't wash your feet," Jesus said, "you have no part of me." These words carry more force than just a few comments about humility or the physical washing of the disciples' feet.

"If you do not allow me to wash your feet, you have no part of me." Some have tried to interpret this statement as a reference to baptism. But it seems to me that this action is a prophetic sign. It points to the redemptive death of Christ. Peter's refusal to have his feet washed is a rejection of the Lord's supreme gift. John is seeking to tell his readers that this act of humiliation is the sign of the One who would wash and cleanse us all by his sacrificial death.

In one of our hymns we sometimes sing about "the fountain filled with blood drawn from Immanuel's veins." We are cleansed as we are plunged beneath "the fountain filled with blood." Foot washing is a sign of the cleansing that Christ gives us through the power of his sacrifice and death. I believe foot washing is much more than a symbol about baptism. Our baptism is a sign of the greater cleansing—the cleansing that Jesus Christ brings through the essential washing of his death. The first requirement of every disciple is self-surrender. We must let Christ serve us—wash us—so we can be clean.

## The Incarnation

John tells us that Jesus was conscious of who he was. He laid aside his outer garments (v. 4). This action was symbolic of Jesus "laying down" his life. "The laying aside of his outer garment" is symbolic of Jesus' incarnation. John states that Jesus knew he had come from God and was going back to the Father. He had laid aside his divinity and come into the world in human form. Laying aside his divinity, Jesus came into the world and took the form of a servant.

## Peter's Response

Peter's response seems to show his growing awareness of who Jesus was. First, he refused to let Jesus wash his feet. However, when Jesus said, "If you do not let me wash your feet, you have no part of me" (v. 8), then Peter went to the other extreme. "Not just my feet," he said. "Bathe all of me, Lord" (v. 9). "No," Jesus replied. "Only your feet need to be washed" (v. 10). It was the custom to have a complete bath before one came to a special meal like the Passover. After one arrived at the house where he would celebrate the Passover, he would then need only to have his feet washed in order to be clean.

## A Sign of Jesus' Death

What was Jesus saying here? I believe that foot washing was a sign of Jesus' death, which would bring redeeming grace to cleanse his followers. Throughout a disciple's life, he or she would need constantly to be cleansed again, because each one would sin again and again. Having experienced the redeeming grace of Christ, we will need to return to Christ to ask him to forgive us again for our other sins.

Jesus said to Peter, "Later on you will understand what I have done" (v. 7). When would Peter understand? Was it when he was in the garden and took a sword and cut off the ear of the high priest's guard? When would he understand? Was it when he denied Jesus three times? Was it when he saw Jesus arrested? When would he understand? Was it when he saw Jesus hanging from a cross and he thought all was lost? When would he understand? Was it when he thought it was finished and said, "I am going fishing again," and returned to his old occupation? When would he understand? Did he understand when he saw the risen Lord? Did he understand when he went out to minister in Jesus' name? Only after the resurrection did he really understand.

## A Sign of a Way of Life

I think this story is also a *sign of a way of life*. Jesus, by taking a towel and a basin, symbolized that those who followed him were called to imitate the way of service. "I have given you an example that you should do unto others as I have done unto you" (v. 15). Does that mean we are supposed to perform foot washing all the time? No, that is not the primary message of this sign. Jesus is our model—our pattern. He has called us to a higher way. We are to imitate Christ. Foot washing is a sign of our call to serve and minister in Jesus' name.

In the Eastern Church there is a tradition for a Maundy Thursday liturgy that dates back to the fifth century. The archbishop enters the cathedral on Maundy Thursday (the Thursday before Good Friday), robed in all of his vestments, accompanied by twelve priests and the reader of the Gospel. After the choir has sung the introits and collects, the celebrant removes his outer vestments, girds himself with a towel, and pours water into a basin. He begins to wash the feet of the priest who represents the disciples. The priest who represents Judas eagerly sticks out his feet for Jesus to wash and kiss. Then another priest who portrays Simon Peter is in tears and draws his feet back in reluctance.

The service concludes with the recitation of the dialogue from John 13 and with the words, "Now you are clean but not all." The archbishop turns and points to Judas. Edwyn Hoskyns, the Cambridge New Testament scholar, states that this ritual drama was not commemorated as an isolated incident in the life of Jesus, nor was it merely an example of humility. "It forms," he believes, "part of the commemoration of the Passion, and the liturgy is dominated by the thought of the Incarnation, the Death, and the Resurrection of the Son of God."[3]

## Set Apart as Servants

Jesus has called each of us to take a towel and basin and go into the world and serve in his name. It may be that when Jesus washed the feet of his disciples, *that acted parable was a sign that they were being set apart as servants too.* "I have given you an example that you should do as I have done," he said. This means, "You are being called to serve as I have been called to serve." Some of the disciples died as martyrs. Their call to service required some of them to lay down their lives for Christ.

In churches where the minister wears a robe and a stole, the stole is not worn merely as decoration. The stole is a symbol of the towel. It is a visible reminder of service. Maybe it would be appropriate for an ordination service of a minister or a deacon to include a foot-washing. The minister or deacon would actually wash the feet of others. This would be a statement that the minister is being set apart, not to be a big shot in the church, but to be a servant.

The church of Jesus Christ, if it really models itself after him, will take the form of a servant. Jesus said, "I came into the world not to be ministered unto but to minister, and to give my life a ransom for many" (Matt 20:28; Mark 10:45). "The greatest of all," Jesus said, "is the servant of all"—that is, "If anyone would be first, he/she must be least of all" (Matt 23:11; Mark 9:35). If his church is authentic, it will model its life after our Lord who took the Suffering Servant as his image. He was willing to lay down his life in sacrifice for us. The church is not to be served or to serve itself but to minister in the world in Jesus' name. Jesus calls us not to see whether we can be big shots but whether we can serve.

On rare occasions, the world seems to attest to this kind of greatness. Many people didn't agree with some of Albert Schweitzer's theology, but nobody could deny that his work as a medical missionary in Africa was more fully modeled after the teachings of Christ than that of many others who considered themselves orthodox. He put service in first place. Maybe one of the finest examples of authentic Christianity in recent years has been Mother Teresa. Even into her eighties, she still arose at five o'clock each day and spent time in prayer, and then she worked among the poor and hurting people in India. These two people understood the meaning of Jesus' image of the towel and basin.

Years ago, when missionaries first went to China, they asked a group of Chinese pastors what most impressed them and appealed to them about the teachings of Jesus. None of them noted his miracles or the words of the Sermon on the Mount. One of them said quietly that the thing that most impressed him was the story about Jesus in the upper room washing the feet of his disciples.

The sign of foot washing calls us to practical service. The Christian life is both prayer and worship, but it is also the bearing and lifting of burdens in the world around us. Let us take the towel and basin and follow our Lord, who served us supremely through his death and calls us to serve and live for him.

# Notes

1. Raymond E. Brown, *The Gospel According to John XII-XXI* (Garden City, NY: Doubleday & Co., 1970), 565.

2. Brian D. McLaren, *The Great Spiritual Migration* (New York: Convergent Books, 2016), 92.

3. Edwyn C. Hoskyns, *The Fourth Gospel* (London: Faber and Faber, 1947), 445–46.

# Chapter 4

# The Sign of the New Birth

*John 3:1-21*

Night had just fallen on the city of Jerusalem. A gentle breeze was moving through the olive trees. A stately, distinguished, middle-aged gentleman walked briskly down the narrow streets. Even a stranger in the city could tell that this was a VIP of Jerusalem. His robe and carriage alone would have given evidence of that. Anyone passing him on the street would have known that this was Nicodemus, a Pharisee, one of the separated ones. He was a member of the Sanhedrin, the supreme court of the land, where he sat in judgment on important religious matters. He was likely wealthy and an aristocrat. As he rounded the corner, he took the steps beside the house that led up to the rooftop where he had made an appointment to talk with Jesus of Nazareth.

## He Came by Night

John says that Nicodemus "came by night" (v. 2). Scholars have speculated for ages why Nicodemus came at night. Some have suggested that he was afraid his fellow Pharisees might see him associating with this itinerant rabbi. Others have stated that he came by night simply because it was a convenient time for him to come. After all, he had to work at his trade during the day. It may also have been a convenient time for Jesus to meet Nicodemus on this quiet rooftop away from the crowds. Nicodemus may have selected this time because rabbis loved to debate theological matters at night. Maybe he had heard Jesus that day and felt such a sense of urgency to talk with him that he came as soon as he could, even in the dark. Or maybe John, the writer of this special Gospel, is simply using night as a symbol. Throughout this Gospel, he contrasts light and darkness and those who are children of light and children of darkness.

Regardless of the reason, Nicodemus came by night. And the Nicodemuses of the ages have come to see Jesus night and day, in the morning and in the afternoon. Nicodemus saw Jesus sitting on the cool side of the roof talking with several of his disciples. He moved across the rooftop and exchanged greetings. Then he respectfully gave Jesus a compliment: "Sir, we know that you are a teacher come from God or else you could not do all of these wonderful signs" (v. 2). The "signs" had been an important factor in bringing Nicodemus to Jesus. Does the "we" mean that he was a representative from the Sanhedrin who had been sent to ask Jesus prearranged questions? Or does the "we" mean that there were others of the Sanhedrin who thought that maybe Jesus was the long-sought Messiah?

Jesus cut through all of the flattery of Nicodemus and drove his point home when he said to this distinguished member of the religious establishment, "You must be born from above" (v. 3). Immediately he placed on this distinguished leader's agenda the necessity of change that must come in his life. *This* man? Yes, even this religious leader must be born from above.

## The Importance of "Must"

The word "must" rings through the teachings of Christ like a bugle call summoning people to obedience. At the age of twelve, Jesus said, "I *must* be about my Father's business" (Luke 2:49). Jesus later told his disciples that he must go to Jerusalem and undergo great suffering (Matt 16:21). John 3:14 records Jesus declaring, "Even so the Son of Man *must* be lifted up." On another occasion, he told Zacchaeus, "Come down from that tree. I *must* abide in your house today" (Luke

19:5). And again, Jesus cried, "I *must* do the works of my Father while it is day, for the night comes when no one can work" (John 9:4). "I must" echoed a feeling of necessity in the life of Jesus.

## Religious Inadequacy

"You must be born from above, Nicodemus," Jesus said. "You must respond to God's radical demand for change." But Nicodemus asked, "How can this be? I am a fifty-year-old man. How can I be born again? How can I start all over?" (v. 4). John's Gospel depicts this great leader of Judaism as unable to understand what Jesus was telling him. John's message was clear to the first-century Christian church: Judaism was inadequate. Even some of the most distinguished leaders of Israel did not believe that Jesus could be the Messiah they were anticipating. Nicodemus probably thought to himself, "I have the law. I am a Pharisee of the Pharisees. Why should I have to undergo this ritualistic act?" He wanted to debate theology and discuss religion. But Jesus was trying to lead him to a commitment.

Like Nicodemus, many today do not understand this reference to being born anew. Many people jeer and sneer at talk about "being born again." The idea of a "born-again Christian" is often the subject of mockery and laughter. When Jimmy Carter was running for president and spoke of being born again, the press and others made it a point of ridicule. Many people are uncomfortable to be in the company of those who want to talk about being born again. They either ignore, deny, reject, or mock the demand from Christ for a new birth. But, as Barbara Brown Taylor observes, "The story of Jesus and Nicodemus freed me from believing I had to know the answer to every question about what it means to be Christian. I gained new respect for what it means to be *agnostic* . . . . when all it really means is that *you do not know,* which according to Jesus is true of everyone who is born of the Spirit."[1] Easy answers to the "why" and "how" of the new birth elude us. Like Nicodemus, we continue to seek further light.

## The Mystery of Conversion

Nicodemus exclaimed, "I don't understand how one can be born again." Jesus declared that this is the great mystery of conversion. We can hear the wind blowing and feel its breeze across our faces, yet we don't know its source. Its origin is a mystery, and it has the freedom to go wherever it desires. We hear its sound and see its manifestation, but its source and activity are a mystery. In the same way, the Spirit of God moves in the lives and hearts of people. His way is beyond our understanding. "Look," Jesus might have said. "Look at my disciples here. Look at Peter, James, and John, and notice how God's Spirit has worked in their lives to make them into different people. He can work the same way in your life. You need to be born of the water and of the Spirit" (see v. 5).

Water likely symbolizes the spiritual life, which God brings about by the "celestial waters" in the birth from "above." Both water and the Spirit are symbolic of God's working within a person's heart and mind. They symbolize the mystery of God's presence. "Yes," Jesus asserted. "Nicodemus, even *you* must respond."

## A Sign of the Immeasurable Love of God

Some might debate whether this conversation with Nicodemus was meant as a sign. After all, these verses do not depict any miracles taking place. But I am convinced that John uses this story as a sign. It is a sign of the miracle God can produce in a human life. This conversation between Nicodemus and Jesus reveals a sign of the immeasurable love and unlimited grace of God. Tucked in this conversation between Jesus and Nicodemus, John gives us one of the favorite verses of all Christians: "For God so loved the world that he gave his only begotten Son, that whosoever believes in him will not perish but have everlasting life" (John 3:16). It is the first verse many of us learn. It is the gospel in a nutshell. This verse has been the gateway for many people to learn about the love of God. It is a sign of the immeasurable grace of God.

If you and I could peer into heaven, this verse would come to mind as we beheld the splendor, majesty, and grandeur of God's love. This verse depicts love as overflowing from the ocean of God's grace. It depicts how that fountain of love has spilled into our hearts and into the world. It reminds us that the source of this love comes from God. Think of how awful it would be to live in the world with a God who did not care. But this verse tells us, "For God so *loved . . . .*" The source of this love is God. The scope is "whosoever." Any person—not just the Jews or the Baptists or some other particular group but *any person* of any race, nationality, or gender, anyone who believes—can experience this grace of God.

## Love as a Gift

And this love of God comes as a gift. You can't earn it; you can't merit it; you can't buy it; you can't keep ritualistic laws to get it. You can't isolate yourself in some secluded place and become holy enough to deserve it. Love comes as God's gift. It is not a demand. It comes to each of us as an offer of God's grace to us. "For God so loved . . . that he gave . . . ." He *gave!*

A young grandson was walking one day with his grandfather. After they had walked a long way into the woods, the grandfather looked down at his young grandson and asked him, "Do you know where you are?" "No, Grandpa," the boy answered. "I don't." They walked a little way further. His grandfather asked again, "Do you know how far we are from home?" "No, sir," the child replied. "I don't." "Well, grandson, I think you are lost." "Oh, no, Grandpa," the small boy responded. "I'm not. I'm with you."

When we have received God's grace, when we have responded to his love, and when we walk with him, we know we are not lost. His love and presence sustain us. His love led God to seek us. Just as our physical birth was a gift of love, so our birth from above comes through the gift of God's love for us.

## The Serpent Sign

John refers to a puzzling sign: the sign of the serpent that was lifted up in the wilderness during the wandering of the Israelites as they followed Moses to reach the promised land (Num 21:9). During their wandering, the people of Israel had become disobedient to God and were being bitten by serpents as punishment. God instructed

Moses to lift up a standard-bearing pole with a serpent on it. When the people looked at this pole, they would be healed of their bites from the serpents. It wasn't the serpent pole itself that gave healing, but it served as a sign. It pointed beyond itself to God. Raymond Brown, the noted New Testament scholar, has observed that the "standard-bearing pole" is literally the word for "sign." He wonders if the sign of the serpent might "be one of the factors that led to the Johannine use of 'sign' for the miracles of Jesus . . . ."[2]

The sign of the serpent being lifted up, Jesus told Nicodemus, is a sign that the Son of Man must one day be lifted up. Jesus declared on another occasion, "And I, if I be lifted up, I will draw all people to me" (John 12:32). The reference to being lifted up points, of course, to Jesus' sacrificial death on the cross. John points his readers to the sign of God's love revealed through the death of Christ. He assures his readers that whoever believes can experience God's grace and enter into a new beginning.

## A Sign of Judgment

John also puts up a warning sign before his readers. The grace of God comes not only as immeasurable love but also as judgment. When a light is turned on in a dark room, it shows us the good features of the room but also reveals other things that we might wish were still hidden, like dirt, trash, or dust. When God's love comes into our lives, it challenges us to respond. But if we do not respond, then we are judged by that same love. It reveals our sins. "He that believes on him is not judged, but he that believes not is judged already" (John 3:18).

## A Sign of New Life

John gives us, in this text, a sign of new life. It is a sign of the life we can have as we begin again through God's grace. Often, we say or hear others say, "Oh, I wish I could be a child and start all over again." Here in this passage, Jesus is telling Nicodemus, as well as you and me, that there is an opportunity to begin anew. But notice that this birth comes from above. It is unfortunate that this verse has been translated into the phrase "born again." The correct emphasis is on the birth from above. The Greek word indicates that the source of this birth is God. This birth is not something you can have happen again by saying, "I think I'll get a new start, folks." The focus is on the birth that comes from God. God's Spirit brings something into you that you have never had before. This is a new kind of beginning whose source is God. Like physical birth, this birth is a gift. The change comes about through an act of God.

In the novel *Uncle Tom's Cabin*, Topsy, a little black girl with a wide grin has just been brought to the home of St. Clair after being purchased on the auction block. Miss Ophelia, St. Clair's cousin, asks the small girl, "How old are you, Topsy?" "Dunno, Misses," she answers with a grin. "Who was your mother?" "Never had none," Topsy responds. "Never had a mother? What do you mean? Where were you born?" "Never was born!" says Topsy.

Never was born! There are a lot of people who have experienced physical birth, but they have never experienced the birth of God's presence that transforms their lives and gives them a sense of radiant joy. Remember that this birth comes from above. It is God's redeeming act.

## The Reality of Sin

John also reminds us of the reality of sin. We need this birth from above because our sins have fragmented us, burdened us, and turned us away from God, others, and our authentic selves. We need to experience God's forgiving, restoring joy. Our attitude toward God and life has become so intertwined with the ways of the world that we no longer understand the awful reality of sin. Almost everything is seen as OK. We speak of slip-ups, problems, mistakes, bad decisions, bad conscience, or some little habit we are trying to overcome, but seldom, if ever, do we speak of sin in our society much today. The lines between good and evil have become blurred.

You may have heard the folklore about the church that couldn't afford hymnbooks, so they decided to accept the offer from a pharmaceutical company to provide hymnals in exchange for putting advertisements in the books. But the church didn't know that the pharmaceutical company planned to mix the words of their ads with the lyrics of the hymns. As the congregation stood up to sing from their new hymnal, they sang:

> Hark! the herald angels sing,
> Beecham's pills are just the thing;
> Peace on earth and mercy mild,
> Two for man and one for child.

We have seen this confusion, haven't we? Too often the world becomes intertwined with our religious perspective and we lose sight of the reality of sin. We begin to think that anything or everything is acceptable. We begin to wink at sin and close our eyes to its effect.

## A Loss of Direction

I think we need this birth from above because our authentic selves have lost their sense of direction. Real direction for life is found in Jesus Christ as Lord and Master. Carl Jung, the noted psychiatrist, has said that the central neurosis of our time is emptiness. This emptiness, I believe, is clearly seen in the fact that many do not know where they are going. They are without direction or purpose. A man once told Samuel Shoemaker, rector in the early twentieth century at Calvary Episcopal Church in New York City, that the best way to describe his sense of his life was that he felt lost. When he talked to other people and described that feeling, they responded, "Yes, that is the feeling I have, too. I feel lost." Christ has come to end our sense of lostness and wandering. In the birth from above through Christ, we find direction and purpose.

Many of us also feel fragmented and pulled in all directions at once. Life seems to be out of control. Psychologist William James once observed that conversion is the uniting of the self.[3] The birth from above, conversion, brings us wholeness. The word "salvation" means wholeness. In Christ we are made whole, complete, full people. His grace brings our fragmented selves together. Salvation is the uniting of our divided selves.

## Driven to Deeper Resources

Who among us also does not have needs that drive us to resources beyond ourselves? Several years ago I sat with a family whose teenage son had been in an automobile accident thirty-two days earlier. He had never regained consciousness. While I was at the hospital with the family, he died. Who is sufficient to face this tragedy? Who is sufficient to sit with a loved one in a hospital and watch them slowly dying from cancer? Who is sufficient to face the death of a loved one who is snatched away by war or accident? At such times, we find that we need the resources of God to sustain us. When we have the birth of God's presence in our lives, it makes all the difference in our ability to meet whatever comes our way. Our need drives us to find God's sustaining love.

## Entrance into God's Family

Birth is the entranceway into the human family. John uses the image of birth to depict our entrance into God's family. When you experience the birth from above, you are a member of the family of God. You are God's son or daughter. You are God's child. "Nicodemus," Jesus seems to be saying, "don't chase the wind. Be a member of the family of God. I want you to understand that I have come to show the way. I have come to be the way to lead you into the presence of God. Through me you can know God directly and experience the power of God's grace and love."

Years ago, when I was a small boy, I would often go with my parents to visit some of our relatives in the country. One of my father's brothers or cousins would take me aside and say, "Let me look at you and see if I can see any of your father in you." As an adult today, I can still remember the warm feeling I had when I heard that question. Isn't that the question that should be asked of each of us who is a Christian? Can any likeness of the Father be seen in you? Is there evidence in your life to show something of God the Father?

We don't know if Nicodemus became a believer or not. He is mentioned only two other times in the New Testament. In one of these appearances, he is pictured standing before the Sanhedrin and trying to keep them from condemning Jesus. "Wait, wait," he says.

"Let's hear this man. Let's listen to Jesus and see whether or not he is from God" (John 7:50-51). Following the crucifixion of Jesus, Joseph of Arimathea and Nicodemus bring a mixture of ointments to prepare Jesus' body for burial (John 19:38-42). Maybe he did become a believer. Maybe he did experience the birth from above that Jesus told him was necessary. We don't know for certain, but we can hope that he did.

The following is probably an apocryphal story, but I like it. A man picked up the newspaper one day and saw his name in the obituary column. He reached for the telephone and called the newspaper and asked, "What is my name doing in the obituary column? I'm alive and well." The editor got a copy of the paper and looked in the obituary column and observed, "Sure enough, it is there! I'm sorry. I don't know exactly what we can do. I'll tell you what. We will put your name in the birth notices tomorrow."

Maybe that is what we all need to hear. We have passed from death to life because we have experienced the birth from above in Christ. Let it happen. It is God's great mystery of grace.

## Notes

1. Barbara Brown Taylor, *Holy Envy: Finding God in the Faith of Others* (New York: HarperCollins, 2019), 168.

2. Raymond E. Brown, *The Gospel According to John*, Anchor Bible (Garden City, NY: Doubleday & Co., 1966), 133.

3. "To be converted, to be regenerated, to receive grace, to experience religion, to gain an assurance, are so many phrases which denote the process, gradual or sudden, by which a self hitherto divided, and consciously wrong[,] inferior and unhappy, becomes unified and consciously right[,] superior and happy, in consequence of its firmer hold upon religious realities" (Lecture IX, "Conversion," in *The Varieties of Religious Experience: A Study in Human Nature* [New York: Modern Library, 1902], 189).

# Chapter 5

# The Sign of the Water of Life

## *John 7:37-43*

### The Feast of Tabernacles

Celebration filled the air in ancient Israel. The Israelites had gathered together for the great annual Feast of Tabernacles. It was a festive time for them. It was a time of remembering how God had brought them safely through their forty years of wilderness wandering. During this weeklong celebration, they lived in small booths to remind them of the tabernacles in which they had lived in the wilderness. Finding water in their forty years of wandering had often been difficult. A part of this celebration focused on the time God provided water for Israel when Moses struck a rock and it brought forth water (Exod 17:6; Num 20:11). Moses had been the instrument for providing the wandering Israelites with water to show God's providential care. The Feast of Tabernacles was also a time of thanksgiving. It was similar to a harvest or our Thanksgiving holiday. In this "season of gladness," the people expressed thanks to God for the bounty of their harvest.

One of the high points in each day's celebration was the ceremony where the priests dressed in their white robes, went at dawn to the pool of Siloam, filled a golden pitcher with water, and processed back up the hill to the temple. The pilgrims, who had gathered for their most joyous feast, followed the priests with palm and willow branches in their right hands and citrus fruit, which symbolized the harvest, in their left hands. The people were dressed in festive clothes, and they approached the temple rejoicing as they sang portions of the Hallel (Pss 113–118).

The Levites sounded a burst on their trumpets as the people reached the top of the hill and went into the temple. Finally, the priest approached the altar and poured the water from the pitcher on the altar. The people would then break forth with shouts of jubilant hallelujahs and thanksgiving for God's abundance. On the last day the worshipers circled the altar seven times and waved their palms in the air. As the water was poured on the altar as a libation, the worshipers expressed their joy to God for his great gift of water.

## Human Thirst

It was at this dramatic moment, John notes in his Gospel, that Jesus stood up and cried with a loud voice, "If anyone thirsts, let him come unto me. And whosoever believes in me, let him drink" (vv. 37-38). Jesus took advantage of this fantastic moment and gripping opportunity to make his pronouncement. The crowd was stirred by the words of this prophet from Nazareth who dared to make such a dramatic claim. "If any person—if any man/woman/child—thirsts . . . ," Jesus cried.

The Eastern people knew about thirst. They lived on the edge of a desert. They knew what it was like to have fine sand eat into their pores, to have hot sand penetrate their nostrils, mouths, ears, and eyes. The scorching wind sapped their bodies of strength. They had seen the bones of animals lying in the desert, bleached white by the wind and sun. They knew the dangers of trying to travel across the desert without enough provisions. They couldn't go into the kitchen or some other place in their houses and turn on a faucet for water. Most of the villages or towns had only one well or spring that furnished water for everyone who lived there. If they took a journey across the desert, they knew its certain danger and made careful provision before undertaking such a trip. Water was precious to people who knew what it was like to be thirsty.

## Spiritual Thirst

Jesus said, "If anyone thirsts." Why does Jesus say "if"? Are there those who deny that they know physical thirst? Are there those who deny that they have a deep spiritual thirst? Oh, yes there are! Some of these people may be reading this book today. Some of them have subdued this thirst with religious ceremonies. Ritualistic coverings of religion have become an end in themselves for these people. They go through the trappings and motions of religion, yet their souls—their spirits—have never been penetrated by the grace and love of God. There are others who cover their thirst by supplanting it with their family, recreation, work, busyness, hobbies, or frivolity. They cover this deep thirst by focusing on these other matters, many of which may be important but do not satisfy the thirst. There are others who ignore or defiantly deny that they have any deep-seated thirst. Others place a veneer of indifference over this longing and close their ears, eyes, mouths, and hearts to God. Something else always demands and gets their attention.

## Our Deep Longings

"If any person thirsts . . . ," Jesus cried. "Anyone!" But you and I know that we all thirst not only for water but also for much more. We thirst for love, acceptance, and understanding. Some thirst for recognition, fame, and knowledge. What is this thirst? It is our deep longing to fill an emptiness within us. There is a vacuum within us that we long to have filled with meaning, direction, hope, and purpose. "If any person thirsts . . . ." We know people who thirst. There is the man who is slowly dying with cancer in the hospital. He knows this spiritual thirst. The wife, who is tending his needs, knows thirst. A couple's marriage is being torn apart, and they know thirst. A high school or college student, or a young person away in the military, struggles with loneliness. He or she understands this thirst. The parents whose teenage son has been arrested know thirst. The daughter caring for her elderly parents knows thirst. The young teenager who is pregnant and the parents whose hearts ache—they know this thirst. In your own life you have felt this thirst, this longing to experience some satisfaction of the deepest needs in your life.

## All People Thirst

"If any person thirsts . . . ," Jesus said. "If *anyone* thirsts . . . ." Anyone! What a universal invitation. You who are burdened with a load of sin are invited. You who feel that your life has been broken with disappointment and failure, the appeal is to you. The invitation is extended to you who are bound by the shackles of alcohol or drugs; to you who have felt the burden of bearing unconfessed sins; to you who have misspent your youth; to you who have poured out rivers of tears for deeds done in the darkness of your past; to you who wear the dark veil of sorrow because of unconfessed and unacknowledged sins; to you who bear heavy burdens of guilt; to you who have hurt families or friends; to you who have forged chains of neglect; to you who wear the sackcloth of regret; to you who have a troubled conscience; to you who wear the black clothes of grief; to you who feel you need nothing yet long for everything; to you who feel a deep, unexplained sadness within; to you who feel weary in body and mind; and to you who are defiantly unwilling to acknowledge your need. Whoever you are, if anyone thirsts, let him or her come.

Some people have been driven into a desert or wilderness place and have groped to understand the meaning of life and why God seemed so distant and remote. Some have been driven to a barren wilderness place, and nothing seems to make sense any longer. In the back corner of their wilderness, they cry, "Is there a God? Where is God? I thirst." Some have known, like our Lord, a cross of isolation and fear and have groped—thirsted—to be satisfied with God's loving presence.

## An Audacious Claim

Jesus lifted up his voice and cried, "If any person, if anyone—man or woman, young or old, rich or poor, famous or commonplace—thirsts, he or she can find water to satisfy that desire." It was an audacious claim. Jesus stood before the worshipers that day and declared, "If anyone thirsts, let him come *unto me* and drink." This was a daring pronouncement. But this was the same Jesus who had asserted at the wedding feast in Cana of Galilee that "I am the new wine." This is the same Jesus who had said that the manna of Moses was insufficient to feed Israel today. "I am the bread of life." This is the same Jesus who said to Nicodemus that the serpent that Israel lifted up in the wilderness was insufficient to bring them lasting healing. "If I am lifted up, I will draw all people unto me." This is the Jesus who now claims that the water that Moses provided by striking the rock in the wilderness was inadequate. "I am the water of life."

## An Invitation from Christ

Jesus extended the invitation to the worshipers: "Come." The image John uses of Jesus where he states that Jesus stood and cried is the same image he uses about John the Baptist crying in the wilderness. Jesus lifted his voice and extended the invitation: "Come. Come, you must receive what can satisfy your thirst." We must be willing to approach Jesus and accept what he offers us.

If we will have our thirst satisfied, it is not enough merely to hear about Christ. The invitation is not just to listen, study, debate, or argue about him. We are to come and approach Jesus and receive. This invitation is extended to all people. "Come unto me, all ye who are weak and heavy laden," Jesus said (Matt 11:28). "He who has ears to hear, let him hear" (Matt 11:15). "Those who hunger and thirst after righteousness shall be satisfied" (Matt 5:6).

## Jesus at the Center of His Teachings

"Come unto me," Jesus said. Jesus put himself at the center of his teachings. "You come unto me," Jesus declared. "I am the one who reveals to you what God's nature is like." This Incarnate One, the Christ, is the one who directs us to God. Jesus said, "I am the one who sustains your life. When you are dying of spiritual thirst, I am the one who satisfies that thirst." This is the same Jesus who said, "I am the way, the truth, and the life" (John 14:6). This is the same Jesus who said, "I am the light of the world" (John 8:12); "I am the bread of life" (John 6:35); "I am the good shepherd" (John 10:11);

and "I am the resurrection and the life" (John 11:25). He put himself at the center of his teaching.

An interesting fact is that there was no fountain of water in the temple itself. The priests and worshipers had to go down the hill outside the temple to the pool of Siloam to get water and then bring it back up to the temple before they could pour it on the altar. In the sacred temple where there was not water, Jesus declared, "I can give you the water of life." Christ is not some nice addition to make life a little better for us. He doesn't just make our lives more attractive or add flavor. He is the one who is able to satisfy the deepest longings and needs of people. He is the absolute necessity for finding a meaningful life. He is the one who quenches our deepest thirst.

One day while Alfred, Lord Tennyson was walking in a garden with a friend, his friend paused and asked Tennyson what Jesus meant to him. He thought for a moment, then bent over and pointed to a flower. "What sunlight is to that flower," he said, "Jesus is to my soul." Jesus is the one who nourishes our souls, quenches our thirst, fills our emptiness, and loads the vacuum of our lives with meaning.

John is telling his readers that there is no life apart from Jesus. The psalmist reminds us, "As the deer longs for the flowing streams, so our souls thirst for God" (Ps 42:1). We are not satisfied until we have drunk deeply from his pool.

When I was a teenager, I used to hike through a beautiful section of the Blue Ridge Mountains of Virginia. We always knew that we would find a cool mountain spring where we could get a drink of water when we reached a certain spot in the climb. (This was also in the days when it was safe to drink from mountain streams.) We would arrive at this cool spot and drink from that pure mountain spring and be refreshed so we could continue our journey. Jesus Christ refreshes our spirits like a cool mountain spring. The water of his Spirit refreshes, cleanses, and preserves us.

## A Summons to Respond

"If anyone comes unto me," Jesus said, "let him or her drink." He summons us not just to hear or listen but also to receive, to drink, to take Christ into our spirits and be nourished by him. When you and

I take Christ into our lives, the one who is "the water of life" preserves us, bringing a quenching rain. Like dry soil in its arid condition, our spirits lie open to God to send the rain of grace upon us and fill us with joy. But the water of Christ is also cleansing. It cleanses us from our sins and "washes us white as snow." It is refreshing. The refreshment of his Spirit gives us such vitality and joy that we experience the real radiance of living.

Years ago in a coal-mining town in England, a noted lecturer spoke to a gathering of citizens. He denounced the church, the Bible, and Jesus. When he finished his speech, he said, "Well, I guess I have shown all of you today how Jesus Christ is really a myth." One of the miners who had come to hear the speaker that night was still dressed in his dirty clothes. He stood up and said, "Mister, I don't know what the word 'myth' means. But I want to ask you one question. Can you explain me?" The miner paused and then he continued, "Three years ago my home was miserable. I drank all the time. I couldn't keep my job, and I mistreated my family. But someone introduced me to the love of God through Jesus Christ, and my whole life has changed. I have stopped drinking. My family loves me. I am able to keep a steady job. Mister, can you explain me?" Jesus Christ comes into our lives, changes us, and fills the void with his presence.

## Christ as the Living Water

Look next at the promise from Christ. Jesus declares, "As the Scripture said, 'Rivers of living water will flow out of his belly'" (v. 38). This promise sounds strange, doesn't it? Scholars have tried for centuries to determine what passage of Scripture Jesus was quoting. Some have suggested that it was from Ezekiel 47:1-11 or from Zechariah 14:8, which states, "On that day, living waters shall flow out of Jerusalem." M. E. Boismard has suggested that Jesus may have been citing a Tarqum or an Aramaic translation of Psalm 78:15-16: "He led forth streams of water from the rock; and he brought down, as it were, rivers of flowing water."[1] We don't know for certain. Jesus often paraphrased some of the Scriptures he quoted from the Old Testament.

This strange promise from Jesus does not make it clear whether those who receive Christ will have this water flow out from them or the water will flow from Jesus. It could be that Jesus is talking about those who accept him. When a person accepts Christ, Christ gives them water within that fills their lives with an ever-flowing fountain. Remember what Jesus told the woman at the well in Samaria: "The water that I shall give him shall be in him a well of living water springing up into everlasting life" (John 4:14).

Other scholars feel that Jesus is referring to himself. The waters that flow out of Jesus as the Messiah give us life everlasting. The image of the belly or the heart are references to the seat of inward desire. John will later state that when Jesus was hanging on the cross, his side was pierced and blood and water came out (John 19:34). He is the one who by his death set "the living waters" flowing for the redemption of humanity. Others have suggested that the Greek word translated "belly" or "heart" could also be translated "cavity."[2] The word "cavity" might provide a link to the rock that was referred to in the Feast of Tabernacles. This rock was the one tapped by Moses until water rushed forth to quench the thirst of the children in their wilderness wanderings. Jesus was clearly declaring himself to be one greater than Moses.

## The Coming of the Spirit

In verse 39 there is a strange statement: "There was as yet no Spirit." I am not certain exactly what that means. It is obvious that the Spirit of God was already in the world. But John is informing his readers that the manifestation of God's Spirit had not fully come until after Christ died. Although the Spirit of God has always existed, the fullness of his presence was not experienced until Pentecost. At Pentecost, the baptism by the water of the Spirit, the power of the Spirit of God came in a way that it had not come before (Acts 2:1-4). As William Barclay observed, atomic power existed long before it was discovered. Human beings did not invent atomic power. It has always existed. Only after it was discovered was it utilized.[3] The Spirit of God has always been at work in the world, but it was manifested and poured out supremely at Pentecost by the sacrifice and death of Christ.

# The Response to Christ

Finally, John notes the response of the people to the words of Jesus that day. Some of the people said, "Why, this man is a great prophet" (v. 40). Others said, "This is the Messiah" (v. 41). The Pharisees wanted the temple police to arrest Jesus, but they had been unable to follow these orders. They said, "Nobody has ever spoken like this man before" (7:37-52). A debate about who Jesus was broke out among the people. "Could the Messiah really come from Galilee— that hick part of the world?" They ended in a division of thought.

When Jesus extends his invitation to discipleship to some people, many end in division. They do not want to respond. They would rather debate, ridicule, argue, or take a particular theological position than commit their lives to Christ. Into the desert of our lives, Jesus Christ comes to offer us the water of life. What he wants from us is not discussion, debate, or argument but commitment.

You may have heard the story about the man who was stranded in a desert and dying of thirst. Another man discovered him and came to his assistance with a canteen of water. As the thirsty man tried to grab it, the man who had come to rescue him said, "First let me tell you about the nature of water. Let me give you the chemical formula for water. Let me tell you about the trip I had to make across the desert to bring this water to you. Let me tell you about the structure of this canteen: its color, description, size, and content. Let me describe for you the cover and contents of this canteen." The thirsty man grabbed the water canteen and cried, "My God, man, give me the water. I *am* dying of thirst!"

There are people in the world who are dying of thirst—spiritual thirst. They are not interested in our theological debates. They are not concerned with our ecclesiastical minutiae. They want somebody to give them the water of life. Jesus Christ stands before you today and cries, "If any man/woman/child is thirsty, let him/her come unto me and drink. Whosoever believes in me, let him/her drink." Come to Christ. He will satisfy your deepest thirst.

# Notes

1. Raymond E. Brown, *The Gospel According to John*, Anchor Bible (Garden City, NY: Doubleday & Co., 1966), 322.

2. See George R. Beasley-Murray, *John*, Word Biblical Commentary, vol. 36 (Waco: Word Press, 1987), 116–17.

3. William Barclay, *The Gospel of John*, vol. 1 (Philadelphia: Westminster Press, 1956), 265.

# Chapter 6

# The Sign of the Light of the World

## *John 8:12; 9:1-16, 30-41*

For those of us who live in this modern world, which is always flashing with multicolored lights, it is difficult for us to comprehend what life was like in the darkness of night during the time of Jesus, especially in the winter. Two thousand years ago, people could not flick a switch and have light. They had little furniture and no television, radio, stereo, fireplace, or books. Poor people were fortunate to have a little light, which came from a burning wick floating in oil or from some burning reeds. In the wintertime, the poor often brought the cattle into a lower level in their homes. They slept huddled together as a family to keep warm. Night was often not a pleasant time.

Night was dreaded not only for its physical problems but also for spiritual reasons. Many believed that demons and devils were everywhere at night. They thought the air at night was filled with them. They feared that demons were behind every rock, bush, and tree and in the sea. John uses night in his Gospel as a symbol of the forces of evil that Jesus Christ came to overcome. He came into the world of darkness as God's light. John illustrates this truth by taking us again to the Festival of Tabernacles.

Earlier he wrote (7:37-43) about this festival and noted that Jesus stood up in the middle of the celebration and made the declaration, "If anyone thirsts, let him/her come unto me." He would provide for them a fountain of life.

## The Feast of Tabernacles

John states that Jesus spoke "again," which notes that this is the second time in the festival when Jesus spoke to the crowd. Did he make his declaration at the moment when the candles were lit? The lighting of candles was a special part of the Feast of Tabernacles. Four huge candle stands stood in the Court of Women with golden bowls sitting on top of them. Young men from the priestly class climbed ladders with jars of oil and poured the contents into the bowls. The wicks were made from the discarded garments of the priests. At a designated moment at night, after the golden bowls had been filled with oil, the wicks were lit and the light would illuminate the court. Young men, who were noted for their purity and piety, would then dance all night before God. The Levites would play their trumpets, harps, zithers, cymbals, and other musical instruments to celebrate God as light.

Was it at the moment when these lamps were lit that Jesus stood up and spoke again at the Feast of Tabernacles? He declared, "I am the light of the world; whoever follows me will never walk in darkness but will have the light of life" (8:12). We don't know at exactly what point in the festival Jesus spoke. But that certainly would have been a magnificent moment for Jesus to make that declaration. Whenever Jesus spoke at the festival, his listeners knew the significance of his words as symbolic of the presence of God in the pillar of cloud by day and the pillar of fire by night while their ancestors were wandering in the wilderness (Exod 14:19-25).

## A Blind Man Symbolizes Darkness

In the ninth chapter of his Gospel, John gives an illustration of how Jesus is the light of the world. This story is another of his "signs." As

Jesus was walking along the road shortly after the Feast of Taberna-cles was over, he saw a man who had been blind from birth sitting near the gate of the temple in Jerusalem. There is no indication in the story that the man knew about Jesus and cried out to him for help. In the purpose of John's Gospel, this man symbolizes darkness. He was blind. Jesus' disciples asked him what to us seems like a strange question: "Who sinned to cause this man's blindness? Did he sin or did his parents?" Remember that this man was blind from birth. We would likely ask, "What kind of sin could he possibly commit?" This question focuses on one of the old rabbinical discussions and debates about whether a child could sin before birth in his mother's womb.

Is prenatal sin possible? Their theological discussions would go something like this: if a pregnant woman entered the temple of a false god to pray and worship, the child in her body sinned just as the mother did. Those who believed in prenatal sin pointed to the struggle between Jacob and Esau, who "wrestled" in their mother's womb before they were born. Their action was depicted as prenatal sin. Others believed in the preexistence of the soul in the garden of Eden. This gave people another opportunity to sin. Such discussions might seem difficult for us to accept today, but they were hot items of debate in ancient times.

## A Representative of Suffering Humanity

The blind man also represents suffering humanity. Too many people who experience suffering in the world simply want to engage in phil-osophical or theological debates about it. "What did I do to deserve this? Why has this come upon me?" they ask. They feel that they must have done something wrong in order for suffering to happen to them. We often hear or express those same feelings. But you and I know that there are a lot of good people who suffer. As William Willimon wrote in *The Christian Century,* "The notion that only good things happen to good people was put to rest when we hung Jesus on the cross."[1] The innocent often suffer. We all may suffer. Sometimes our pious phrases freeze on our lips when we try to express them in the face of cancer, disease, sufferings, and grief. Easy answers fail us in the dark shadows of ignorance, pain, and war. Suffering is a reality in the world. God doesn't cause suffering, but God does permit it. All suffering is not the result of your sin or my sin. Suffering is simply a part of the world in which we live.

Jesus told his disciples that through this man's blindness, God could be glorified. Whatever our suffering or pain is can be an occasion for the glorification of God. This does not mean God sends suffering upon us to bring glorification to himself. But human pain and sorrow can be opportunities for the manifestation of God's mercy. Sometimes the way a person bears his or her suffering reveals the glory of God. Jesus declared. "We must do the works of God while it is daylight, because with darkness comes death, and we will not be able to work" (9:4). Live out your life—whether in joy or sorrow—as an occasion to show God's grace. These opportunities will not last forever.

## The Guiding Power of the Light

Notice next the guiding power of the light of Christ in this passage. Jesus put clay, which he had moistened with saliva, on the blind man's eyes. He then told him, "Go and wash in the pool of Siloam" (v. 7). When translated from Greek, the word "Siloam" means "sent." Some scholars have seen Jesus represented in this passage as "the spiritual Siloam"—the One who washes people clean."[2] The blind man goes to the pool of Siloam. From this same fountain, the blind man received his sight. His steps to the pool symbolized his obedience, and healing came to him because he obeyed. He responded to Jesus' guidance and went and washed his eyes in the pool, and he was able to see.

God often tries to give us the guidance of his presence, but we cannot always comprehend it. The listeners in Jesus' day would not have missed the point when Jesus said, "I am the light of the world." The occasion for the lighting of the candles during the Feast of Tabernacles reminded the Israelites of how God had led them through the wilderness. At night God's guiding presence was "a pillar of fire," and by day he had been "a pillar of cloud" (Exod 13:21-22). This Shekinah (a rabbinic euphemism for God as present among humankind) cloud had guided them through the wilderness for forty years. In his declaration Jesus was saying, "As God guided you in the past, I am now the One who will furnish you light to guide you through life. Whatever wilderness you are in, I am the One who will guide you through it."

## Looking for God's Guidance

I have often wished that God guided my life by some kind of visible light that I could always see. If you have ever been camping in the woods on the backside of some mountain where there are no electric lights, you are always glad to have a flashlight to throw a beam in front of you to give you a lighted pathway in which you can walk. I have often prayed, "God, why can't you give me a light—a visible sign—like that?" I don't know about you, but I have never had that kind of clear direction from God. I have never had God provide a visible light for my path. I have sensed the guiding light of his presence within. God works quietly within our hearts and minds to guide us. He works through other people and opportunities we have. He guides us through inner inspiration and illumination. God does guide us. He will direct our path. But we need eyes to see and ears to hear. He will not give us further light until we respond to the light we already have.

## The Reaction to the Blind Man's Healing

Note next the visible effect of light. Jesus, after healing the blind man, disappeared from the scene for a while. The attention of the story focuses on the man who was born blind and was now able to see. His neighbors began to ask if he was really the same guy who had been blind. "It looks like him," they said, "but we are not sure. He can now see" (vv. 8-9). They had seen him sitting by the temple gate for years with his "tin cup" extended as he begged of those who passed by. Now he was walking around, and he could see!

The Pharisees asked the former blind man's parents, "Is this really your son? We don't like what he is saying about this Jesus who healed him. We are probably going to cast him out of the temple." His parents didn't want to lose their status in the religious community, so they responded, "He is old enough. You ask him what happened.

We don't want to get in any trouble. We want to be able to attend worship and not be excommunicated. You ask him" (see vv. 18-23). The Pharisees interrogated the man again and asked him to tell them about how he was healed. He related his experience about being blind from birth and how a stranger came along one day and healed him. "Give God the glory. We know that this man is a sinner," the Pharisees cried. "A sinner?" the former blind man asked. "Only good people can do miracles like this. It is not possible for a sinner. He is a prophet." He then asked them if they were questioning him a second time because they wanted to become disciples of the healing man. "Give God the glory," they cried. "He can't be a prophet," they declared. "Moses is our prophet. We are his disciples." Here again Jesus is set in opposition or set in a superior position to Moses and the law.

The religious leaders then asked the man to repeat the whole story again. Was this an attempt to confuse him or catch him in some statement they could use to discredit him? He repeated the story again. Finally, in disgust he stated boldly, "I don't know what you are talking about. All I know is that I once was blind and now I can see. This man did it! Nobody has ever heard such a marvelous thing. If this man wasn't from God, he couldn't do anything." They then cast him out of the temple. This means that they excommunicated him. He was "unchurched," as some say in the Baptist tradition. (See vv. 24-34.)

## A Story the Early Church Clearly Understood

What a marvelous story this must have been for the early church! This man represented what many of the first disciples had experienced. Many of the first disciples were Jews. When they declared that Jesus was Lord, their neighbors didn't understand their decision. They often didn't want to have anything to do with them after they took this stand for Christ. Sometimes their parents would disinherit them. The religious leaders often criticized them openly, sanctioned them, and sometimes excluded them from the temple. They were called heretics and experienced rejection and alienation from family and friends. This story of the blind man was a mirror of their own struggles. They knew firsthand the dangers of taking a visible stand for Christ. Many of them had been persecuted for such a stance. This was their story too.

## What about Rejection Today?

This kind of rejection doesn't happen much today, does it? I wonder why. When we, like this former blind man, meet Jesus Christ, our Christian walk should be a visible one. You may have heard the story about a lumberjack who was converted in a revival meeting. When it came time for him to return to his lumber camp, he grew concerned and talked with his pastor. He wanted to know what he should do and how he should act when he returned. His pastor encouraged him to try to live the Christian life. Later the pastor met the lumberjack again and asked, "How did it go?" "Wonderful," the lumberjack replied. "Nobody ever found out I was a Christian!"

Isn't that often the case today? If you are a Christian, others should know it. The Light of Christ is meant to be shared with others. If it is genuine, we cannot hide the light. If we go into a dark room and strike a match, the light cannot be hidden. As long as the match burns, the light will shine in the darkness. It will be visible. It cannot be hidden.

There is an ancient legend about the conversation between the sun and a dark cave. "Come up into the light and see the sunshine," the sun said. "I don't know what you mean," the cave replied. "There isn't anything but darkness." When the cave did come out, he was surprised to find light everywhere.

The cave then said that he wanted to show the sun his darkness. "I don't know what darkness is," the sun said. "Come down into my cavern and you will know what darkness is," the cave responded. One day the sun came down into the cave and said, "Show me your darkness." When the sun was there, there was not darkness but only light.

When Jesus Christ enters your life, you should give off light so others can see that you are his disciples. Jesus said, "You are the light of the world" (Matt 5:14). We reflect his light. The light we have experienced in Christ will be visible in all that we do. One morning a small child noticed a beam of light that was cast across the floor through a dining room window. She stepped into that beam of sunlight and looked up at her mother and said, "I am standing in the smile of God!" When you and I have experienced the sunlight of God's love and are bathed in his glory, grace, and radiant joy, how can we keep it a secret? That light will shine!

## Steps in Spiritual Development

Go a step further and observe the revealing quality of the light in this story. Although the blind man was able to see instantly, notice the slow, unfolding process in his knowledge of who Jesus was. This man ever so slowly moved up the steps of faith.

In this man's conversation with the Pharisees, we hear him acknowledge first of all that Jesus was a man. "The man Jesus made mud . . . ." Later he affirmed that Jesus was a prophet—not *the* prophet but *a* prophet. Boldly he attested to his own experience with Jesus: "I don't know anything about your theological arguments," he was saying. "I only know that I was once blind and now I am able to see." After he was cast out of the temple, he met Jesus once again. Jesus asked him, "Do you believe in the Son of Man?" This was clearly a messianic claim. The man who had been blind asked, "Sir, who is he? Tell me that I might believe in him." Jesus said, "I, who am speaking to you, am he." "I believe," the man said, and he fell down and worshiped Jesus. He began by seeing Jesus as a man and then as a prophet. Next he declared his own experience with Jesus, and finally he ends in adoration before Jesus. (See vv. 35-38.)

Hasn't that often been your pilgrimage and mine? When we were young, we may have understood Jesus as our friend. Later we understood him as a man, as a teacher, as a prophet who was sent by God. Finally, we recognize him as Lord and Savior. There are usually steps in our spiritual development. Few people, if any, instantaneously understand fully who Jesus Christ is. For most of us, it is a lifelong pilgrimage to try to understand who Jesus really is.

# Jesus at the Center of His Teaching

Jesus did not hesitate to put himself right at the center of his teaching. "I am the light of the world." "I am the one who reveals to you what the nature of God is." "I am the one who illumines your way." "I am the one who guides you." Christ himself is the light. He says "I *am* the light," not "I give you light." This is not indirect light but the direct light of his presence. He gives light by being who he is. We come to him as the light to receive his light. As the Incarnate One, he brings the "fullness" of the light of God's presence in his person. This astounding claim is a ringing declaration that he alone points us to God. And men and women through the centuries have found it to be so. Jesus is indeed the One who guides us to God.

In Holman Hunt's famous painting *The Light of the World*, Jesus is depicted standing and knocking at a wooden door with a lantern in his hand. There is light coming from the lantern. To me, there is a mistaken image conveyed in that painting. The rays of light come from the lantern. The light should come from the presence of Christ. He is the light. He is the one who illumines our hearts and minds and leads us to God.

# The Light Is Also Life

There is another step in this journey to understand the nature of Christ as the sign of light. John tells us that the light of Jesus Christ gives us life. Whoever follows Jesus Christ will not walk in darkness because Christ is the light of life. "He who follows me will never walk in darkness but have the light of life" (8:12). Just as physical life cannot exist without the light of the sun, spiritually we cannot exist apart from Christ's light. I know you have at some time kicked over a discarded board and noticed what has happened to the vegetation underneath the plank when it was cut off from the light of the sun. It is distorted, white, twisted, dying, or dead. Vegetation needs light. In a similar way, our lives are dependent on the light of God's presence. As we open our lives to him, we experience real life and authentic meaning. Our lives issue from the source of life—the light of God that we experience through Christ. Our response to this eternal light brings us life. "This is life," John says, "to know the Son"

(John 17:3). Eternal life doesn't begin when we die. For the Christian, he or she has this life now as a present possession. When death comes, we continue in our relationship to God that began when we became his children.

## Light Brings Judgment

But observe finally that our text declares that whenever light comes, it brings judgment. If you could go with me into my study on a dark night and turn on the light, the light would reveal what is there. You would see several chairs, books on the shelves, and likely a cluttered desk with books and papers stacked high. This light might also show a trashcan that needs emptying. It might show muddy footprints on the carpet. Light will illumine. The light will show whatever is there, the good and the bad.

When God's light comes into our lives, it first comes as judgment before it is experienced as grace. When Jesus met this blind man, the man knew he was blind. He didn't argue, "Well, I can see. I don't need you." He had been blind since birth. When Jesus offered him the opportunity to see—to be cured, healed, and made whole—he obeyed. He found healing and redeeming love. His blindness was gone, and he was able to see.

The Pharisees in this story symbolize those who are spiritually blind. They thought they already knew everything there was to know about God. They are the "know-it-alls" in this story. Notice how often "we know" resounds in this account. "We know this man is a sinner." "We know that God has spoken to Moses." Sometimes people cannot experience God's revelation and the light of his grace because they are blind through "know-it-allness." These Pharisees thought they could see but were really blind. "This is the judgment, that the light has come into the world, but men loved the darkness more than the light because their deeds were evil" (John 3:19). The sin of blindness that John pictures here is of not believing in Jesus as the Christ. The light of Christ first comes in judgment. We acknowledge our sins and ask forgiveness. If we accept his love, the light of his judgment leads to grace and to the warm, redeeming light of his presence.

Years ago in Arizona, there was an old prospector who had a cabin on the edge of a desert. He had the only well in that part of the state. Each night he would hang a lantern outside his door. Some people would criticize him and say, "Why do you waste your oil that way?" Late one night, a knock came on his door. He went to the door and found a man who was almost dead from thirst. The man had seen the light off in the distance and had walked through the desert toward it. Finally, he fell on the porch and begged for water. That light saved his life and led him to the place where he could get water.

Two thousand years ago, God's lantern was lifted up in the darkness of the world, and all people were invited to find the path to life through its light. The cross of Christ has cast its rays down through the centuries. Christ is the light of the world. He continues to draw men and women to that light. As we respond to the One who is the light of life, we find redemption and eternal life.

One of our hymns expresses that truth this way:

Come to the Light, 'tis shining for thee;
Sweetly the Light has dawn'd upon me,
Once I was blind, but now I can see;
The Light of the world is Jesus.

Come to that light. You will find redemption and eternal life.

## Notes

1. William H. Willimon, "When Bad Things Happen," *The Christian Century*, February 22, 1989, 199.

2. George R. Beasley-Murray, *John* (Waco: Word Press, 1987), 155.

# Chapter 7

# The Sign of the Good Shepherd

## *John 10:1-18*

Many of us who grew up in cities, and even some who have lived in rural areas, may have never seen a sheep. All we know about sheep we have learned from Christmas pageants or from ordering a leg of lamb. But most of us are unfamiliar with sheep. When our children were small, we took them to visit a farm that belonged to one of our church members. Our son Bill told one of his friends later, "I saw a real, live peacock—in person!"

## The Importance of Sheep in Ancient Times

I expect there are a lot of folks who have never seen a live sheep "in person." The rural images of ancient Israel are unfamiliar to most of us. Even the people who still raise sheep today use methods that are far removed from the ancient Eastern practices of keeping sheep. There are more than five hundred references in the Scriptures to sheep, rams, or lambs. Sheep were the chief livelihood—the major wealth—of the people in ancient times. When someone asked a man how wealthy he was, he would respond by telling how many sheep he had. That was his way of measuring his wealth.

In biblical times, sheep provided meat and milk. From sheep wool the people got yarn to make clothes. The skins of the animals were sometimes used by shepherds for outer garments, with the wool side turned in during cold weather. The skins were also used to make tents. Meat and horns from the sheep were used in the people's sacrificial system of worship. Much of the life of the ancient nation of Israel was built around sheep. Sheep were a part of their everyday lives. When Jesus drew upon the images of shepherd and sheep, his listeners of some two thousand years ago knew intimately the meaning of these pictures. But for many of us today, the symbolism may not be quite as clear.

## The Background for this Sign

Let us try to capture something of the setting of the story in which Jesus depicts himself as the good shepherd. Jesus' saying that he was "the light of the world" and "if anyone thirsts, let him come to me" were made against the backdrop of the Feast of Tabernacles. The Feast of Dedication was likely the background for his "good shepherd" image. John 10:22 makes a clear reference to that particular feast. The Feast of Dedication was a memorial celebration of the purifying and rededication of Israel's temple that was accomplished in 164 BC by Judas Maccabeus and his family in reaction to the desecration of the temple under Antiochus Epiphanes. On the Sabbath nearest the Feast of Dedication, there was a practice of reading biblical texts about sheep and shepherds in synagogue worship. Most likely Jesus made his pronouncement in a context when those Scriptures were clearly in his listeners' minds so they would understand fully this particular reference.

Some might wonder why I picked this text as one of the signs of Jesus, because there is no miracle related with this story. But I am convinced that this passage is connected with the healing of the blind man. The "parable" about the sheep and the shepherd follows that sign and continues to serve as an interpretation of it. The blind man, after he received his sight, was excluded—excommunicated—from the temple. Jesus assured this man about a new relationship that was greater than the temple. The sign of the good shepherd communicates to this healed man and to us something special about God. It is a sign of new hope, a sign of encouragement as well as judgment.

## A Divine Claim

When Jesus declared, "I am the good shepherd" (v. 11), I am convinced that John expected his readers to sense that this was a divine claim. In the Old Testament, there are more than eighty references in which God is depicted as the shepherd of people. There is, of course, the familiar one from the Twenty-third Psalm, "The LORD is my shepherd." Psalm 95:7 notes, "For he is our God, and we are the people of his pasture, and the sheep of his hand." Isaiah 40:11 declares, "He will feed his flock like a shepherd. He will gather the lambs in his arms. He will carry them in his bosom, and gently lead those that are with young." The words from Ezekiel 34 would have already been read in the synagogue, and this powerful description seems to be the source for Jesus' words on this occasion. The following are some of the words that the people would have already heard.

> These were the words of the LORD to me: Prophesy, man, against the shepherds of Israel; prophesy and say to them, You shepherds, these are the words of the Lord GOD: How I hate the shepherds of Israel who care only for themselves! Should not the shepherd care for the sheep? You consume the milk, wear the wool and slaughter the fat beast, but you do not feed the sheep . . . . Now I myself will ask after my sheep and go in search of them. As a shepherd goes in search of his sheep when his flock is dispersed all around him, so I will seek out my sheep . . . . I will feed them on good grazing ground, and their pasture shall be the high mountains of Israel . . . . I myself will tend my flock, I myself penned them in their fold, says the Lord GOD. I will search for the lost, recover the straggler, bandage the hurts, strengthen the sick, leave the healthy and strong to play, and give them their proper food. (Ezek 34:1-3, 11-12, 14, 15-16)

## The Genuine Shepherd

In these passages and others, God is depicted as the shepherd of his people. Jesus drew on these declarations and used them to point to himself as the good shepherd. Jesus said, "I am the good shepherd." "Good" is probably not the best translation of the Greek word used here. The Greek word can mean real, beautiful, excellent, competent, noble, perfect, model, or example. I like best the word *genuine.* "I am the genuine shepherd."

The genuine shepherd is distinguished from the claims of the false shepherds. Jesus had indicated earlier that he was the pure water, the actual light, the real bread, and the better-quality wine. Jesus declares here that he alone is the genuine shepherd. The Book of Hebrews calls Jesus "that great shepherd of the sheep" (Heb 13:20). Peter speaks of Jesus as "the shepherd and bishop of our souls" (1 Pet 2:25). In the book of Revelation there is a reference to Jesus as "the Lamb which is in the midst of the throne" who "shall be their shepherd and guide them to the fountains of life" (Rev 7:17). The claim to be the good shepherd is a divine claim. The scribes and Pharisees knew clearly what this assertion by Jesus meant, and that is why the text states later that they tried to arrest Jesus (John 10:39). They knew what he was claiming. They clearly saw this as a messianic claim

## A Willing Sacrifice

Four times in this chapter Jesus states that the genuine shepherd will lay down his life for the sheep (10:11, 15, 17). The phrase "lay down his life" is John's picture of the voluntary death of Jesus. His death was not forced upon him, but it was his willing part in the redemptive process that God had ordained (10:13-18). John carries this view of "the smitten shepherd" forward as Jesus is crucified on the Passover as the "Lamb of God." Unlike hired servants or robbers, Jesus genuinely cares about the sheep. He willingly gives his life for them.

The words "all that came before me are thieves and robbers" (v. 8) follow the prophetic denouncement of false and unfaithful spiritual leaders (John 9:35-41). Here it is most likely a reference to the religious leaders who had excommunicated the man who was born blind but whom Jesus healed. The scribes and Pharisees are depicted as the hired men—thieves and robbers—while Jesus is the genuine shepherd who models what a real spiritual leader should be.

# Guidance from Psalm 23

## "Shall Not Want"

As the genuine shepherd, Jesus Christ will lead his sheep. We see the images of God as a shepherd guiding his people in many Old Testament passages, especially in the Twenty-third Psalm. David declares, "I shall not want" (Ps 23:1). In that ancient land, which was so desolate, it was easy to experience want. It was the responsibility of the shepherd to guide the sheep to find food. Sometimes the shepherd had to search endless miles through a vast wasteland to locate good feeding grass for the sheep. But the shepherd knew where the grass was and carefully guided his sheep to it.

The ancient Israelites knew something about hunger and thirst. The shepherd declared that he would not want because there was a God who would guide him toward food. The Psalmist was assured of physical satisfaction by God, but more than that, he knew that his own spiritual needs could be satisfied. When he hungered and thirsted after righteousness, he had the assurance that God would comfort him and sustain him.

## "Green Pastures"

The sentence "He makes me lie down in green pastures" is a colorful one (v. 2). Green is the most restful of all the colors. For the shepherd of that day, it was a difficult task to guide the sheep to good grass because it was found only in a few selected places. The noonday heat would beat down on the rocks with such intensity that one could not even put his foot on one without getting burned. The shepherd would lead his sheep into the shadow of a mighty rock or hillside where they could find a place to eat and rest. A shepherd knew that his sheep would not eat and rest unless they were free from fear, pests, and tension. It was the shepherd's responsibility to lead his sheep to a place where they could have these freedoms and enjoy the comfort and security of a green place. The shepherd labored to find and maintain such a place. The sheep were quieted by the shepherd's presence as he guided them to the green pastures.

## "Still Waters"

"He leads me beside the still waters," the writer continues (v. 2). The sheep were frightened by rushing streams. They would not drink from water that was moving very fast. They were afraid that their wool would become saturated with the water and they would drown. The shepherd knew that he had to guide the sheep to "still waters"—a place of safety, serenity, and security.

## "Restores My Soul"

The sentence "He restores my soul" (v. 3) means basically that God brings one back from wandering. The sheep might go wandering off and get lost, and the shepherd would have to go searching for it. It was always dangerous for a sheep to wander off. Sometimes an unscrupulous shepherd might build a pit and place sticks, grass, or limbs over it, and because sheep are so nearsighted, one might not see the trap and stumble into the pit. The sheep could then be captured and slain by the person who found it. Jesus once told the Pharisees that they should set aside their laws about the Sabbath if a sheep fell into a pit on the Sabbath day. "He restores my soul" declares that God brings the sheep back from its wandering.

## "Paths of Righteousness"

"He leads me in paths of righteousness" has an interesting meaning (v. 3). In the biblical age, a shepherd could not say, "If you want to know something about me, call the place that I worked last," or "Ask them to send a letter of reference," or "Here are my credentials." A shepherd was known by his ability to lead and care for his sheep. His reputation as a good or bad shepherd was known throughout the community.

A shepherd did not go behind the sheep; he literally went before the sheep, and they followed him. His reputation was made or broken by his ability to walk up a mountainside, find the pathway that was safe and secure, and have the sheep follow him up the mountain, down the trail into a valley, toward water, or toward grass. "He leads me in paths of righteousness," because I have experienced him as the

God of righteousness. He is Jehovah God—the God we can trust. His reputation is good. You and I can commit our lives in trust to the eternal Christ, who has revealed to us what God is like. We have seen that he is a righteous God, a loving God, and one that can be trusted indeed.

### "The Dark Valley"

Even when we walk through the "dark valley" (v. 4), we have the assurance that God is with us. The shepherds in ancient Israel, and even today, often led their sheep through deep ravines and dark valleys. The sheep would begin to be nervous as they approached the dark ravines. These ravines were often the place where the sheep were attacked by wild animals or robbers who would rush down the hillside and try to steal the sheep or hurt the shepherd. It was the shepherd's responsibility to lead the sheep safely through the dark, difficult valley to the other side.

With Psalm 23 as a "backdrop," let us move to the words of Jesus John 10 to offer us a path through life. We will at times transition back into the guidance from Psalm 23 as it enriches our insight into John's Gospel signs.

## "Jesus as the Door of the Sheepfold"

Jesus said, "I am the door of the sheepfold" (John 10:7). "I am the gateway. I am the one through whom you come to find good pasture." One enters through him to be fed and nourished. He is the one who provides fullness of life. The gate is for the sheep. Jesus is the gate to salvation. "I am the way, the truth and the life," Jesus said. "No one comes to the Father except through me" (John 14:6). Some see in Psalm 118 a reference to this sacred gate: "This is the gate of the LORD; the righteous shall enter through it" (v. 20). Jesus is seen also as the gate through which the shepherd enters to be with the sheep. The thieves and robbers, Pharisees and Sadducees, try to enter some other way.

In ancient times a sheepfold might be located in several places. Sometimes a shepherd would lead his sheep back home to his small village where the sheep would be placed in a sheepfold that was built right next to the shepherd's own house. A door was constructed in the fence so the sheep could enter through it and be corralled beside their owner. At other times a shepherd would guide his sheep into a cave at night for safety. If the shepherd were in a wilderness area, he would lead his sheep to a tableland and construct a type of "fort" around them. He would make a circle of rocks stacked on top of one another until they were several feet high. He would then place briars on top of the rocks to keep wild beasts from climbing over them.

At night, the shepherd would call the sheep in one by one, and they would pass under the rod that he would stretch across the doorway. As each sheep passed under his rod, he would examine them to see if they had any cuts or bruises. If so, he would pour oil in their wounds and then let them into the sheepfold. After the sheep were safely in the sheepfold, the shepherd would sleep in the doorway. He literally became the door. If any intruder tried to get to the sheep, they had to come through him. He was the door. Jesus said, "I am the door. I am the way. I am the good shepherd."

On other occasions the shepherd would build a fire in the doorway so no one could get into the sheepfold. When Jesus said, "I am the door," his listeners understood this image. Jesus was asserting, "I am the way for you to have fellowship and communion with God. I am the avenue—the entrance through which the real teacher or shepherd comes. I am the doorway by which you test every teacher and disciple. I am the legitimate door through which the real teacher enters. I am the genuine door. I am the one through whom you pass to find abundant life." Jesus is the way to God.

## The Shepherd Knows His Sheep Personally

As the genuine shepherd, Jesus also gathers his sheep personally to him. In ancient biblical times a shepherd would sometimes brand his sheep by cutting a notch in their ears. This would be his way of identifying them as his property. When others saw this notch, they knew to which shepherd the sheep belonged. The psalmist was reminding us that God has his mark on us as his children. He knows us personally. He is our personal shepherd.

Our society often seems unconcerned about people. Do you get weary with the lack of personal concern all around you or feel like you are known only as an account number? We need to renew our interest in one another, to learn each other's names.

We struggle to be known as people—to be accepted as individuals. But a shepherd of biblical times knew his sheep individually. Often a shepherd gave his sheep descriptive names like "brown foot," "black ears," "long snout," or "wanderer off." D. T. Niles once told a story about a young shepherd lad who was asked how many sheep he had. "I don't know," the lad said. "I can't count." "You can't count?" the man asked. "How can you keep count of your sheep then?" "Oh," the shepherd lad said, "I know them by their names. And if they wander off, I simply call them by their names, and they come back." Even today in Palestine, I am told that several flocks of sheep might be intermingled at night into one fold. The shepherds will sleep until the next morning and then go to the sheepfold and call their sheep. As each shepherd begins to travel away from the fold, the sheep that belong to him will follow. If it looks like the sheep are going to follow the wrong shepherd, he calls out to the sheep. When they hear his voice, they recognize it and follow him.

## David Reminds Us of the Importance of the Personal

David had this personal sense of God's presence. Note the personal assurance in the Twenty-third Psalm: "The LORD is *my* shepherd. *I* shall not want. He maketh *me* to lie down . . . He leadeth *me* . . . He restoreth *my* soul . . . *I* will fear no evil. Thy rod and staff comfort *me* . . . Thou anointest *my* head with oil" (KJV). On and on goes the emphasis on the personal. The heart of our religion is in its personal pronouns. God directs his concern toward you and me. Jesus said, "I know my sheep and they hear my voice and they follow me." There is a sense of individuality in God's knowledge of us. Jesus assures us that we are not lost in the vastness of humanity. God knows us individually and gathers us to himself. God gathered not just Israel, Jesus said, but other sheep as well. Jesus has reached out to the Gentiles and across the centuries to you and to me. Now we too are a part of his church.

### "Your Rod and Staff"

But as the good shepherd, Jesus also guards his sheep. In ancient biblical times a shepherd had little equipment, but he used it skillfully. Most of the time he had a small bag made of skin in which he would keep his food—his lunch—that he would take with him into the field. He also would have a slingshot.

You remember David and his slingshot, of course, and how he used it as his weapon against the giant Goliath. A shepherd always carried a sling. It was used sometimes to ward off wild animals. Sometimes the shepherd used the sling to throw a stone right in front of the nose of a sheep as the animal began to wander off, as though to say, "Listen here, buddy, you had better come on back here. I don't want to go looking for you."

The rod, or club, was the shepherd's weapon of defense. We even use the expression today to talk about a gun as a rod, an instrument of power. The rod was an instrument of power for the shepherd. The shepherd would find a small sapling and dig up part of the root with a knot in it. He would work with the wood until it became hard and powerful. He could kill a snake or sometimes even a bear with it. It became his mighty weapon to help defend the sheep against animals and other enemies. In the day of David, Israel still had hyenas, bears, lions, panthers, and other wild beasts that threatened the lives of the sheep. He had to be ready to protect them against all dangers.

The staff is the long stick with a crook on the end that is so familiar in our Christmas pageants. For the shepherd, this was an important piece of his equipment. He would use it to reach out to a wandering sheep, grab the sheep by the leg, and pull him back from his wandering into the flock. Sometimes, if there was a young animal in the flock and if the shepherd put his hands on it, he knew that the mother would no longer have anything to do with it. He used his staff to reach that animal and draw it back. Sometimes he would use the staff to ford a creek or to reach up and knock down green branches from the trees so the sheep might have something to eat.

On other occasions, he would use the staff to clear the grass of snakes or other things that might be dangerous for the sheep.

Often the shepherd would simply stick the staff upright in the ground, put his outer garment over it, and then lie down under a tree and take a nap. The sheep were so nearsighted that as long as they could see his garment there, they would think the shepherd was still standing nearby. This gave him an opportunity to get a brief snooze. The staff was indeed an important instrument to the shepherd. To David, the rod and staff were symbolic of the protection and comfort of God. God is our rod and staff. We know that we can depend on God for our strength, power, fortification, and comfort.

### "You Anoint My Head with Oil"

The shepherd tenderly cared for the sheep. The sheep also had to have its head anointed. This anointing, in ancient times, was primarily a mixture of olive oil, sulfur, and spices that was poured on the nose of the sheep and rubbed in to protect it from flies and the other pests that annoyed it. If this were not done, the sheep would get a disease called scab and become unfit. This disease could be so painful to a sheep that it would butt its head against a tree or rock in an attempt to gain relief. When the Scriptures say that only an animal without blemish could be sacrificed, this usually meant a sheep without the disease called scab. The shepherd would anoint the sheep's heads and prepare them so that they would not have to worry about pests and could eat and graze in comfort.

Jesus is telling us that as sheep of the good shepherd, we can be assured of his tender loving care. Remember, the tender shepherd senses all of our needs. We can hear him say, "I know your pain. I know your hurt. I know your problems and difficulties." In Jesus Christ, we have seen a God who cares. As the shepherd, Jesus symbolizes both strength and tenderness. In Jesus Christ the good shepherd is the symbol of caring love. He comes as the "Encourager." Wayne Oates writes, "Encouragement means putting heart into people. It means giving them strength for the living of this day. . . . By the power of the Lord Jesus Christ, I bring to you a ministry of encouragement. I want to come alongside you to brace you up."[1] Christ stands with us to assure us that we are never alone in our pain, exhaustion, frustrations, trials, needs, or anything we encounter along life's pathway. He is always beside us.

## A Friend to the Sheep

The shepherd was indeed a friend to the sheep. God is our friend and we can run to him for strength. The words "shepherd" and "friend" come from the same Hebrew root. Moses was described as a friend of God. Enoch walked with God in friendship. Jesus said, "I no longer call you slaves, but you are my friends." We all reach out to people and long for someone who will be our friend.

The sheep found a great friend in the shepherd. If you are not familiar with sheep, you might not understand the expression "cast down" in regard to sheep. This expression is used to describe a sheep that would lie down or burrow itself too deeply into the grass or soil and get on its back so it could not stand up by itself. The more the sheep struggled, the worse its situation became. It was literally "cast down." When the sheep was on its back, its body developed some internal gases that also made it impossible for it to stand. In that position, the sheep was absolutely dependent on the shepherd to set it upright again. If the sheep had wandered away from the other sheep and found itself in this "cast down" condition, it was easy prey for buzzards and wild animals. Can you imagine the sense of joy the sheep experienced when it saw the shepherd coming? On finding the sheep in the "cast down" position, the shepherd would speak tenderly to the animal, caress it, slowly roll it on its side, and gradually get it back on its feet while rubbing its legs and body to restore the circulation.

Who among us has not been in some "cast down" position? Sometimes our spirits are low, and we might feel crushed down or feel that life is hopeless. We see ourselves as victims who are at the prey of all the buzzards circling over us. But be assured that none of us is alone because there is the good shepherd who loves us, cares for us, and comes to our assistance. The one who said, "I am the good shepherd" cares for us. These words were directed to the blind man who had just received his sight from Jesus and then had been excommunicated from the temple. Jesus assured him with the words, "Remember, I am the shepherd. I am the real teacher—the genuine shepherd. The other teachers—the scribes and Pharisees—are thieves and robbers. They are false teachers. Don't let their words or decisions bother you. I am the One who presents to you the true path, the true way to God. Do not be frightened by what others have done to you. I am the way, the truth, and the life." Remember, when you experience difficult or low moments, be assured that you have the presence and power of God to sustain you and bear you up. So take hope and have courage today.

Henry Drummond was a famous Scottish minister who lived in the twentieth century. He was visiting friends one day in the hills of Scotland. His host told him that they were not going to accompany him to the village to catch the train. "Our coachman is a wonderful man, but he has been defeated by drink," his host said. "We hope you may have an opportunity to say something that will help him."

Drummond got up on the seat by the driver of the coach. After a short while, Drummond had won the man's confidence. The man was soon bearing his soul to him. He told him about his difficulties, struggles, and failures. As they continued to ride along, Drummond said to him, "Suppose, as we ride along these curves and hills, the horses you are driving got out of control. Then you realize you cannot manage them. In a flash, however, you recall that the man who sits beside you is the finest horseman in Scotland and that there has never been a span of horses that he could not control. What would you do?" "Oh," exclaimed the coachman, "is that what Christ expects me to do?" "Exactly," said Drummond. "Turn the reins of your life over to him!"[2]

## Let Christ Direct Your Path

Let Christ guide you. Let him be the One to direct your path. Let him be the One who gives your life guidance and strength. As the good shepherd, Jesus Christ is the One with whom we place the reins of our lives. He is the One who guides us, loves us personally, and guards us. He guards our very souls. We know that when we are in his hands, nothing can snatch us out of them because his love is supreme. His power will sustain us.

I love the mistranslation a small girl gave of the Twenty-third Psalm when she said, "The Lord is my shepherd and that's all I want!" Indeed, it is! When the Lord is our shepherd, the good shepherd, what else do we need?

## Notes

1. Wayne E. Oates, "The Ministry of Encouragement," in William Powell Tuck, *A Pastoral Prophet: Sermons and Prayers of Wayne E. Oates* (Macon, GA: Smyth & Helwys Publishing, Inc., 2017), 36.

2. F. W. Boreham, *A Lark Sings* (London: Epworth Press, 1949), 201–202.

# Chapter 8

# The Sign of the Bread of Life

## *John 6:1-14, 26-35*

The story of Jesus feeding the five thousand must have been one of the favorite tales in the early church, because it is the only miracle recorded in all four Gospels. John's version of this story was likely one of the most popular accounts. Its popularity has continued through the ages, most likely because of the reference to the boy and his lunch. The sixth chapter of John is the longest chapter in his Gospel. The chapter has a central theological theme and is divided into two sections. The first part focuses on the miracle, while the second is a discourse or sermon about the miracle.

### The Miracle of the Loaves and Fish

Let's begin by looking at the miracle. Jesus was tired and weary from his demanding ministry. He had just received word that John the Baptist had been beheaded. He crossed the Sea of Galilee by boat to get away from the crowd. He hoped to get some rest for a few days. The Sea of Galilee is a small lake. It is only about thirteen miles long and eight miles across. The crowds, who had followed Jesus on one side of the sea, walked around the lake to the other side or took small boats across to hear Jesus preach. John indicates that it was Passover time. Many pilgrims may have been traveling to Jerusalem. A great crowd of about five thousand men gathered by the seaside to listen to Jesus. The women and children were not included in the number. The crowd was likely much larger than five thousand.

The story tells how Jesus received the lunch from the small boy, blessed it, and distributed it to the crowd of people. After the crowd was fed, twelve baskets of leftovers were taken up. Scholars have wrestled with the meaning of this miracle for centuries. Some have tried to dismiss it by putting the focus on sharing. The small boy shared his lunch with Jesus, and that unselfish act inspired everybody else to share their lunches. They all shared with those who did not have any food, and this made everyone feel good. But that interpretation is not satisfying to me. I do not believe that the Gospel writers would have recorded this story if the message focused primarily on people sharing their lunches with those who didn't have them. The Gospel writers were convinced that something extraordinary had happened here.

## An Unlikely Resource

Let's look at this story and see if we can capture something of the essence of the miracle and then the meaning or sign to which it points. Jesus discovered food for the crowd from what you and I would call an unlikely resource. Help came from a small lad with five barley loaves and two fish. Barley was usually the food of a poor person. The two fish were likely pickled. At that time, people had no other way of keeping fish fresh.

Jesus has worked with unlikely resources through the ages, hasn't he? He has utilized people like you and me and many others. He has called boys and girls, men and women into his service who appeared to be unlikely resources. They may not be the most intelligent or the most gifted. They often do not seem to be the sources you and I might choose. But here beside the Sea of Galilee was a lad who was in the right place at the right time and who was willing to meet a need. God has always been able to find those who would serve him. Look at Abraham, Moses, David, Esther, Ruth, Elijah, Jeremiah, Mary the mother of Jesus, Peter, James, John, Paul, Billy Graham, Mother

Teresa, and countless thousands of others who appear to be unlikely resources.

There always seem to be voices like that of Philip who say, "Well, what is one lunch among so many folks? It would take a working man's wage for a year to pay for this crowd to eat" (see v. 7). That is literally how we might interpret Philip's estimate of what it would cost to feed the crowd. There are always people who point to the church and its Christian disciples and say that they are an inadequate resource. They feel that the church can't possibly change the world with its limited resources. These people continually ask, "How can we possibly do in the world what needs to be done for God?" We all appear to be unlikely resources. So some want to give up and walk away. Some say, "Why try? We don't have enough people or the right kind of people." If you and I had looked at the twelve disciples who gave their all to follow Jesus, we might have asked, "How in the world can his church ever amount to anything?" But that "insignificant" group of men turned the world upside down for Christ.

The answer to whether or not this inconspicuous group could accomplish anything is symbolized in the lad who willingly gave his resources to Jesus. He used what he had. These questions are always raised: "What are they among so many? Who are they to serve Christ? What can this person with limited gifts possibly do?" Unselfishly, the lad shared what he had.

## Jesus Blesses and Uses All Resources Committed to Him

When you and I give our resources to Jesus, it is amazing what he is able to do with them. If you and I give him our intellect, our gift of music, our athletic ability, or whatever our talents are, his touch can transform them. As he blessed the barley loaves and fish, Christ's blessing on our gifts exalts them. The ancient Stoics had a saying that even the lowly earthworm serves God. Is it not true that all of God's creation serves God? Service to God is not restricted to the most exalted people, like presidents or world leaders. Privates as well as generals serve in the army. Each person who commits his or her resources to God is used in his kingdom.

When the lad's lunch was placed in the hands of Jesus and he blessed it, it was multiplied and Christ was magnified. I am not going to try to debate the "how" of the multiplication of loaves and fishes. The New Testament never deals with the "how" of it. The writers simply proclaim it.

But deep down, you and I know. We have seen this kind of miracle before. We have seen how Christ could take a resource that seemed to be inadequate, limited, or useless, touch it with his grace and power, and see it transformed. We have witnessed cities transformed, people changed, and lives made different because Jesus Christ touched them with his spirit. Christ is glorified as people *really* serve him. That is, they do not seek to magnify, glorify, or uplift themselves but point beyond themselves to Christ so he might be glorified.

## Grace Enough for Others

When Christ is glorified, there is always grace enough left over to be shared with others. Some scholars have said that the twelve baskets taken up after the meal symbolized the twelve tribes of Israel. The message was that Christ had enough provision to feed all of Israel! God's gift through Christ is adequate to feed all people. Jesus didn't come simply to meet our essential needs. He came to give us abundant life. God's grace will abundantly pardon us. Christ's message reveals that God's grace is abundant enough to forgive all who will response.

## The Response of the Crowd

Look at the response of the crowd to this miracle. It is the response we see so often when physical needs are met. They want the person to keep giving them bread. The crowd exclaimed, "He is a prophet. Let's make him a king. Let's make him president of the world. Let's put him in charge of taking care of us" (see vv. 14, 34). Their physical needs were met, and they wanted this person to keep meeting those needs. They had gotten from him what they wanted—food—and they wanted to keep using him for their selfish wishes.

Unfortunately, we have seen evidence of this same goal in too many churches. Some preachers and laypeople throughout the ages have proclaimed that Christianity and the church of Christ will meet all of our physical needs and even make us rich in ways beyond our imagination. This false doctrine is expounded from too many pulpits today. Jesus is "used" as a means to acquire fame, wealth, and health. But this is not what Jesus promised those who followed him.

In his autobiography, Phil Donahue tells about an experience he had in Holden, West Virginia, when he was a young reporter for CBS. There had been a cave mine disaster, and twenty-eight miners were trapped deep in the darkness of the earth. For three nights Donahue and others waited in the bitter cold for the miners to be rescued. Cameras and crews from around the country waited to see what would happen. Fortunately, the miners were rescued. They gathered around smudge pots to warm themselves in the snow and cold. The mining town preacher asked the rescued miners and their families to gather around the smudge pot to pray and sing. The miners and their families joined hands and sang "What a Friend We Have in Jesus." Then the preacher led them in a prayer.

Donahue said everybody was moved by this beautiful scene. It gave him goose bumps. He knew that it would make a great film for CBS, but the camera was frozen, and they were not able to record it! When the cameras thawed out at 2:30 in the morning, Donahue said he went over to the preacher and said, "Reverend, I am from CBS News. Would you please go back through your prayer again? We have 206 television stations across this country who will hear you pray for these miners." "Son," the old mining preacher said, "I just couldn't do it. I have already prayed to my God, and any further praying at this time would be wrong. No, sir, I just can't do it."

Donahue was shocked and got on the telephone to New York and reported, "That blankety-blank preacher won't pray!" But Donahue said that the preacher's stand was the finest example of moral courage he had ever seen. This man was unwilling to do Christianity and Jesus as "showbiz." He would not sell his soul, even for CBS.[1]

But whole hosts of people today want to do religion as theatrics or entertainment. When religion is treated this way, it places the focus on the preachers and away from Christ and turns the church into a theater. Too many want Jesus for selfish ends. Religion is simply a way to be a "star" and get rich.

# The Interpretation of the Miracle

Now let's look at the second part of John 6, which focuses on the discourse, or interpretation of this miracle. You won't like this part. It has stuck in the throats of readers down through the ages. Scholars have tried to interpret this discourse basically in three ways. First, they have seen it as an emphasis on the incarnation of Christ, the one who came in the flesh. Second, they have seen it as dealing with the mystery of the Eucharist, the sacrament, or as you and I would say, the Lord's Supper. Third, they have seen it as an attempt to deny that the Eucharist—the Lord's Supper—has magical dimensions.

### Bread Is the Staff of Life

What is John trying to tell us in this sermon or discourse on the miracle? Jesus delivered this discourse the next day in the synagogue in Capernaum. Let's begin our attempt to understand what Jesus was saying about the sign of the bread of life by noting that bread is the staff of life. Philip had asked earlier, "How can we buy enough bread for these people?" Jesus did not want to send the people away hungry. He was concerned about physical needs. Jesus taught us to pray, "Give us this day our daily bread." Bread—physical food— is essential for life and health. Jesus knew that if an individual was hungry, before you could talk to that individual about his or her spiritual condition, he or she must first be fed.

A vital part of the essential ministry of the church is to feed the hungry. Studies indicate that 500 million people are starving right now. 800 million are living in absolute poverty and suffer from hunger and malnutrition. Nearly one in four people, 1.3 billion people in the poorest nations, live in extreme poverty with an annual per capita income less than $1 per day. One out of every eight children in the United States under the age of twelve goes to bed hungry every night.[2] We have difficulty understanding this when we always have more than enough to eat and often wrestle with dieting. But the church *must* be concerned with the hungry in the world.

## Spiritual Hunger

Second, this sign reminds us that there is a deep longing for satisfaction from more than physical food. Physical food alone will not sustain us. We look for something beyond or beneath our physical drive. "You must work," Jesus said, "not for this perishable food, but for the food that lasts, the food of eternal life" (6:27). We have to look for something that sustains the soul. Jesus points us beyond our physical drives. Ultimately, food, sex, drink, ambition, and our possessions cannot satisfy. We are driven to something deeper in our lives. "Our hearts are restless," Augustine prayed, "until they find their rest in you." This is the hunger beneath all hungers. When Jesus was tempted by Satan to turn stones into bread, he responded by saying, "Man does not live by bread alone" (Matt 4:4). We are driven to find the sustaining power that goes beyond the physical.

## Christ as Our Spiritual Sustenance

Third, this sign points to Jesus as the bread of life to affirm that he is our sustenance. Jesus declares that it is he who furnishes the real food that will last. Jesus appears to engage in a dialogue with the Jewish people about Moses. Their argument went this way: "Moses gave us manna in the wilderness. You performed a miracle across the lake and fed five thousand people. Show us another miracle. Moses provided food for the children of Israel every day. Can you keep on giving us food like Moses did for forty years? If you can do that, then maybe you are really the Messiah" (see v. 30). A popular tradition held that before the new age dawned, a prophet like Moses or Elijah would appear at Passover and "feed" Israel as Moses had fed his people.

Jesus said, "Two things are wrong with your interpretation. You have bad exegesis. Number one, it wasn't Moses who gave the manna. The 'he' refers to God. It was God who gave Israel manna, not Moses. Second, the correct emphasis should not be on 'he gave' but on the Father who 'gives.' *He gives.* God is the source of the bread, and he continually gives this heavenly bread." (See vv. 32-33.) Jesus also stressed that it was "my Father" who gave the true bread.

"I," Jesus said, "am the bread of life" (v. 35). "I am" echoes through this Gospel more than twenty times in different places. Most scholars are convinced that this is a divine claim. "*I am.*" Jesus places himself at the center of his teachings. What Christ does cannot be separated from who he is. Both are linked together. We cannot take the teachings of Jesus apart from the Christ the Son of God. They are interwoven.

## The Eternal Bread

The Gospel of John continues, "For the bread of God is that which comes from heaven and gives life to the world" (6:33). Christ is the One who has come to us from God. He is not just any man. He is "the man." He is the bread from above—the One through whom God has revealed himself in his highest and fullest sense. "Jesus turned religion and history on their heads," writes Richard Rohr, "inviting us to imagine that God would give *himself as food for us!*"[3] This summons us to a deeper awareness of God's love for humanity.

As Fred Craddock observes, this sign points beyond "bread to Bread."[4] Jesus is the "Bread" of life. Through him, God's Spirit sustains us, nourishes us, feeds us, and enables us to have the abundant life.

Jesus also says that the bread he gives us will sustain us forever. The bread of Moses was eaten by the children of Israel and they later died. But here Jesus assures them, "This is the bread which comes down from heaven, that a man may eat of it and not die" (6:50). The bread that Jesus gives is living bread. The reference to "coming down from heaven" (v. 33) indicates the reality of the incarnation. We know that the disciples who believed in Jesus did later die. But we do not really understand the words of Jesus if we associate them only with this earthly life. The bread that Jesus gives is eternal food. It nourishes our inner being, our soul. It fortifies the spiritual person so that he or she has eternal life through Jesus. "This is eternal life, to know the Son" (John 17:3). To be in the Son gives us life so that even death does not separate us from him.

## The Scandal of this Sign

The Jewish people, who listened to the words of Jesus, were scandalized at this teaching. A fierce dispute arose among the Jews about the meaning Jesus gave to his sign: "I am the bread of life." "How can this man give us his flesh to eat?" they asked (see John 6:53ff). Jesus replied, "In truth, in very truth, I tell you, unless you eat the flesh of the Son of man and drink his blood you can have no life in you. Whoever eats my flesh and drinks my blood possesses eternal life, and I will raise him up on the last day. My flesh is real food; my blood is real drink" (vv. 52-55). Now, if you and I don't understand those words, the Jewish people of Jesus' day surely didn't. They were scandalized by them. No Jew would drink blood! Many people have wrestled with the literalism of these words. If we cling to a rigid literalism here, then we will all become believers in transubstantiation—the idea that the elements in Communion literally become the flesh and blood of Christ.

If not this, then what did Jesus mean by the offering of his flesh and blood on this occasion? Most scholars say that this is a reference to the Eucharist, the Lord's Supper. But I like the interpretation I read by Markus Barth, the son of the famous theologian Karl Barth. Markus observed that the word "eat" in this text is an unusual Greek word. It literally means "chew." To chew often means "to eat with joy and pleasure." He concluded that John 6:51-58, and really the whole sixth chapter, "speaks of the incarnation and sacrifice of Christ rather than of the Eucharist."[5] He feels that these are Eucharistic only in the sense that they provide a reason for us to give thanks to God.

You and I never really take Christ into our lives until we acknowledge him as the Incarnate Son. The words about his flesh and his blood are references to his incarnation and sacrificial death. When we begin to "eat" Christ in this way, it means that we assimilate him; we take him into our very being. Just as food cannot help us physically until we eat it, so Jesus Christ cannot really affect our lives until we take his spirit, his life, his words, and his teachings and assimilate them and incorporate them into our hearts. Open your heart—your being—and let him come in. Let him nourish your soul.

## Assimilating Christ into Our Lives

This teaching in John 6 has scandalized many people because they have refused to accept the cross. Paul said the cross was "a stumbling block for the Jews and foolishness for Gentiles (1 Cor 1:23). It is still a stumbling block for many Christians today. These people prefer the popular Jesus; they want the peace-of-mind Jesus. Most people would rather have the Jesus who will make them rich and never challenge their prejudices. But John, along with Paul, attests that we can't have Christ without the cross and still have the real Lord. If we are going to assimilate the real Christ, we must take the One who died for us, the One who came down from heaven. We must respond to One who was incarnate, who literally became flesh. Flesh and blood point us to the incarnation. The Incarnate One laid down his life and shed his blood so that we might experience real life. John affirms that the Christ who died was a real man. He did not merely pretend to be a man. The Son of God who died was a real man.

## A Hard Saying of Jesus

Many were offended by this saying of Jesus and began to murmur. Their murmuring was like the murmuring of the children of Israel in the wilderness. They murmured that this saying was "hard to tolerate." John is trying to show the similarity of the present Jews to those who followed Moses centuries before.

John then notes that after hearing this "hard saying" of Jesus about eating his body and drinking his blood, many began to shun him. They turned away and walked no more with him (see v. 66ff). Some of his followers said, "We don't want anything to do with this guy. He is not going to feed us. There are no free meals here. He is not going to keep us rich and happy. He is not going to give us comfortable times. He is going to make us uncomfortable." Some of Jesus' disciples also walked away. He asked his disciples if they were also offended by his words. "Are you scandalized by them?" Jesus asked. "Will you, too, walk away?" (See v. 67). Many, John said, except the twelve, no longer followed Jesus.

Jesus did not hesitate to put the cross at the center of his teaching. He challenged his disciples to "take up their cross" and follow him. Rather than challenging discipleship, many today want a church that will always make them comfortable. They do not want the Christ who challenges their prejudices. They do not want the Christ who calls them to take up their cross and follow him. Unless we have the Christ and his cross, though, we really do not "feed" on the One who is the bread of life. The Christ we have to assimilate is the Christ who laid down his life on the cross for us. If this Christ is going to make a difference in our lives, he must first be allowed enter our lives.

## A Call to Respond

Many of you have received prescriptions from your doctor for various medical problems. You can stand there all day long and read the prescription on the label on your bottle. But your prescription is never going to do you any good until you take it, is it? A lot of people will listen to theories about Christ. They may sit in church or Sunday school classes and hear sermons and Bible lessons, but all of this listening will never do any good until they let Jesus Christ come into their lives and feed on him. Draw him into your being. Let him in to nourish you with his grace.

Another one of my favorite paintings of Christ is Warner Sallman's *Christ at Heart's Door*. With a lantern in one hand, Jesus is patiently knocking on the door with the other hand. Jesus is surrounded with an aura of light and darkness falls behind him. There is no latch on the outside of the door. It is obviously on the inside. Jesus stands at the door and knocks. He wants to come in and sup with the person on the other side.

### Notes

1. Donahue & Co., *Donahue* (New York: Simon and Schuster, 1979), 66–67.

2. See Foy Valentine, "Hunger's Face and Hunger's Faces," *World Hunger Awareness/Action Guide* (Nashville: The Christian Life Commission, 1985), 8–9.

3. Richard Rohr, *The Universal Christ* (New York: Convergent Books, 2019), 131.

4. Fred Craddock, *John* (Atlanta: John Knox Press, 1982), 53.

5. Markus Barth, *Rediscovering the Lord's Supper* (Atlanta: John Knox Press, 1988), 94.

# Chapter 9

# The Sign of the Lamb of God

## *John 1:29-34; 19:28-37*

A small boy's mother referred to her son in front of company as her "little lamb." He looked up at her and exclaimed, "I don't want to be your lamb. I want to be your tiger." In our culture, lambs normally symbolize innocence, weakness, softness, something to be cuddled, or something that provides wool or food. But in the New Testament the reference to the lamb, especially as denoting Christ, is a unique and powerful symbol.

### John the Baptist

Notice the beginning point for this reference in the New Testament. John the Baptist arrived on the scene of the Jewish nation like a tornado. His voice thundered denunciations against the scribes and Pharisees and the hypocrisy of many of their religious practices. He stood in the Judean wilderness and pointed to Jesus Christ. "Behold," he said pointing to Jesus, "the Lamb of God who takes away the sin of the world" (1:29). John, the desert preacher, was the son of a priest. He had often witnessed his father sacrificing lambs in the temple. The image of the sacrificial temple lamb may have been in his mind when he said these words about Jesus.

## The Lamb as Suffering Servant

John the Baptist likely drew from a familiar ancient biblical image
when he pointed to Jesus and said, "Behold the Lamb of God." But
the roots of this image, which he saw reaching back into the Old
Testament, were not the usual metaphors used to depict the Messiah.
The typical images for the Messiah were shepherd, ruler, lion, and
especially king. But John had read Isaiah and some of the other
prophets who noted that the Messiah was to be the Lamb of God, a
suffering servant. His image was drawn from the deep spiritual well
of the fifty-third chapter of Isaiah, where we read these words:

> He was despised, he shrank from the sight of men, tormented and
> humbled by suffering: we despised him, we held him of no account, a
> thing from which men turned away their eyes. Yet on himself he bore our
> sufferings, our torments he endured, while we counted him smitten by
> God, struck down by disease and mercy; but he was pierced for our trans-
> gressions, tortured for our iniquities, the chastisement he bore is health
> for us and by his scourging we are healed. (Isa 53:3-5)

The fifty-third chapter of Isaiah is one of the great passages in
the Old Testament about the Suffering Servant. To whom does this
passage refer? Some have seen it as a depiction of the suffering of
the nation of Israel. Others have seen it as a collective figure for one
or several of the great Jewish prophets. Without question, the New
Testament writers saw it as a prophecy of Jesus Christ, the One who
laid down his life on the cross. The lamb in Isaiah's image (see Isa
53:7) stood before the shearers as the rejected and despised One who
laid down his life for others.

## The Paschal Lamb

John's Gospel not only seems to draw upon the Suffering Servant
figure of Jesus as the Lamb of God but also utilizes the image of the
Passover lamb as a reference to Jesus. According to John's Gospel,
Jesus was crucified at about noon (John 19:14). This was the time
of day when the lambs were sacrificed in the temple for the Passover.
It seems clear that John is picturing Jesus as the paschal, or Passover, lamb. Paul, in 1 Corinthians 5:7, one of the earliest writings

in the New Testament, declares, "Christ our paschal lamb has been sacrificed."

In New Testament times, Passover was a solemn feast. It was observed in the temple in Jerusalem with the sacrificial blood of sheep sprinkled on the altar. The observance continued in each house where the family gathered together for the Passover meal as a time to remember God's deliverance of them from bondage in Egypt. The youngest family members asked, "Why is this night different from all other nights?" Then their families shared with them the story of how God's angel of death had passed over the houses of the Jewish families whose doorposts were smeared with the blood of a sacrificial lamb and how the angel of death touched the firstborn of the Egyptians as the tenth plague of God on Egypt (Exod 12:1-13). John draws images from this feast that was a historical commemoration as a means of focusing on Jesus' death as the true Passover sacrifice.

John uses another image that would have reminded his readers of the Passover when he writes about the sponge filled with vinegar that was lifted to Jesus' lips on a hyssop stalk while he was on the cross (19:29). In Exodus, the Hebrews dipped a hyssop reed in the blood of their slain lamb and then wiped the blood on the doorposts of their houses. The mere mention of hyssop would remind the Hebrew people of the Passover lamb.

## The New Paschal Lamb

In Luke's Gospel account of the Last Supper, when Jesus eats the Passover meal with his disciples, he makes a startling declaration to them: "When you gather for this meal in the future, do this in remembrance of me" (Luke 22:19).

"Now wait a minute, Jesus," the disciples might have thought. "We don't understand." For centuries the Jewish people had observed this meal in remembrance of their freedom as slaves in Egypt. Jesus was asking them to let this meal be a time of remembering something new. He was the new Paschal Lamb. "In the future when you gather to observe the Passover," he was saying, "come to this table for the Lord's Supper and remember the sacrifice I have made for you." That was a revolutionary thought for those faithful Jewish disciples. It is almost like asking us to celebrate America's Independence Day by forgetting that this day was originally set aside to focus on our historic independence from England and the founding of our country. It's like asking us to think about the Fourth of July not as a national holiday but as the beginning of the church. That would be a radical interpretation. What Jesus was asking the disciples to do was like that. He was saying, "Forget your heritage. Remember *my* sacrifice for you."

## The Lamb of God

John the Baptist said, "He is the Lamb of God." Jesus was not just any lamb. He was the incarnate Lamb. In another image from the New Testament, John on the Isle of Patmos declared that Jesus was "the Lamb slain from the foundation of the world" (Rev 13:8). "God was in Christ," Paul wrote, "reconciling the world unto himself" (2 Cor 5:19). Jesus Christ was not just an innocent victim. He said, "No one takes my life from me, but I lay it down of my own free will" (John 10:18). He gave his life as a willing sacrifice. The sacrifice came as God's gift to us. "For God so loved the world that he gave his only begotten son" (John 3:16).

The incarnate love, which we saw in the sacrificial death of Jesus, was not the first time God became loving. For centuries God had tried to reveal his redemptive love to Israel. Israel continually spurned God and turned away from him. Hosea, Job, Isaiah, Jeremiah, many of the Psalms, and other Old Testament writings reveal the way God had tried to disclose his redemptive, caring love to Israel. For centuries God has disclosed his love but with little response from people. At the cross of Jesus, planted on a hillside outside of Jerusalem two thousand years ago, men and women can see the eternal nature of God's love revealed in history at a particular time and in a definite place. God did not suddenly become loving in Jesus. He has always been a God of redemptive love. The sacrificial death of Jesus was the historical manifestation of that eternal love. It was, to use H. Wheeler Robinson's words, "the temporal realization of the eternal cross of God Himself."[1]

# The Sin Bearer

"Behold the Lamb of God," John the Baptist cried, "who takes away the sin of the world" (John 1:29). "Sin" is a word we don't like to mention much today. It seems to me that there are at least three attitudes toward sin in our culture. One approach is to make light of sin, ignore it, or pretend it doesn't exist. We could consider the flagrant marital infidelities or other moral failures of our politicians; often other politicians (and many citizens) seem to believe we should ignore what a public figure does in his private life. That's no one else's business, they said. Some politicians said that if we took ethical standards too seriously, we would have no politicians. Are we to assume that all politicians commit adultery? Are all politicians heavy drinkers? Do they all engage in dishonest practices? Is behavior for a public figure merely a private matter? Our society has too quickly and easily moved to a time when "sin" is denied, ignored, or seen as a normal way of life. Many do not consider anything they do as sin. It's just a part of being human, they said, and doing whatever you feel like doing. A long path down this road can only lead to destruction.

One of the constant dangers with sin is that we trivialize it and focus on matters of little or no consequence. I heard about a prayer meeting that was held several years ago. Various people at this meeting were thanking God for delivering them from certain sins. One woman said, "Thank God. He has saved me from smoking. I have been saved from that sin. Thank God I have also been saved from drinking and from the theater." The following day, her pastor went by to visit her to follow up on her conversion. "I was pleased to hear what you said in prayer meeting last night. I didn't know you smoked. I'm glad you have been released from smoking." "Oh, I never smoked in my life," the woman said. "Well, you have been freed from the terrible habit of drink and we can rejoice." "Never has a drop passed my lips," she declared. "Well," her pastor continued, "I was certainly pleased to know that the temptation of the theater no longer holds you." "But pastor," she exclaimed, "I have never been inside a theater in my life!" Here was a woman who thanked God for saving her from alleged sins that she had never committed! But her pastor left her house wondering why she could not be saved from being the worst gossip in the community. We often trivialize sins by thanking God that we don't commit certain acts. The biblical doctrine of sin is not focused on that at all.

## The Burden of Sin

There are other people who have such a consciousness of their sins that they are overwhelmed by burden and guilt. They are crushed by their load of guilt and can't get free from it. Some of these people need to seek professional help to experience forgiveness and acceptance. Guilt hangs on them like a layer of dust, and they feel dirty and long to be clean and whole.

In a *Peanuts* comic, Charlie Brown has his head bowed down in his hands as he sits on a log. He exclaims to Linus, "Life is just too much for me. I've been confused right from the day I was born. I think the whole trouble is that we're thrown into life too fast. We're not really prepared . . . ." Linus looks at him and asks, "What did you want . . . a chance to warm up first?"[2]

That's what we would like, isn't it? We would like to have a chance to warm up first. We think that would keep us from feeling overwhelmed by the extent of our sins. But life does not give us that kind of opportunity.

## The Radical Nature of Sin

The New Testament speaks of sin as radical separation from God, ourselves, and other people. John the Baptist stressed *sin*, not just individual or particular sins. He heralded, "Behold the Lamb of God who takes away the sin of the world." Our sin is separation, fragmentation, and brokenness. Our separation is from others, from God, and from our authentic selves. Our awareness of our sin pushes us to examine the depths of our being and the meaning of our existence. Sin is a deeper problem than our sins. Sins are a manifestation of our sin. We are estranged from our very being. Salvation fulfills our longing to be made whole, to be brought home from our wandering, to have our emptiness filled.

Many often have a casual attitude toward salvation because they have a weak concept of sin. Why did Jesus have to die on the cross?

Because the sin of humanity was so radical that it caused trauma in the heart of God. His holy nature cannot abide sin's presence. Our sin separates us from God's holiness. Only a radical change can permit us to exist in his presence. Only a change in our nature will allow our separation to be overcome. Our sin is so costly in its effect on God and his created order that only God can overcome its consequences. The effects and implications of humanity's sin are so extensive that only our holy God can atone for them and restore the broken relationship that sin created. God took sin so seriously that only a radical act on his part for his creation could atone for the costly consequences of our sinful fall.

## Remember Your Fall?

Do you remember your first sin? Carlyle Marney, who was talking one day with a group of ministers, was asked about the fall of humanity in the Genesis account. "Where is the garden of Eden?" someone inquired. "Oh," Marney answered, "the garden of Eden is located at 215 Elm Street in Knoxville, Tennessee." The man said, "You are lying! It's somewhere in Asia." "Well, you couldn't prove it by me," Marney replied. "I remember it well. There at 215 Elm Street, when I was a boy, I stole a quarter out of my mama's purse. I went down to the store and bought some candy and ate it. Then I was so ashamed that I came back and hid in the closet. There my mama found me and asked, 'Where are you? Why are you hiding in the closet? What have you done?'"

Where was your first fall? When did you fall? Do you remember it? Do you recall the time when you first became aware of your sin? In that moment, we knew separation, lostness, and brokenness. We knew that we needed a redeemer. Do you remember the address and date of your fall? Even if you can't remember, you know your fall happened. Our sense of separation—of sin—is too real to forget.

Anyone who takes sin casually has never really been aware of the depths and consequences of sin. Talk to someone whose spouse has committed adultery and ask him or her about the casualness of sin. If your teenager walks in the front door and is pregnant or has impregnated someone else, sin is no longer a casual matter. The odor of sin cannot be covered by cheap perfume. The problem of evil and sin in the world is too great. Sin is like a tar baby. Every place you touch the tar baby of sin, you find yourself stuck worse than before, and the more you struggle to free yourself, the more engaged you become. We need a redeemer to set us free.

## The Lamb Bears Our Sin

"Behold the Lamb of God" the Baptist cries, "who takes away our sin." Jesus bears our sin on himself. It is like someone bearing a pack on his back. Jesus is the One "who was delivered for our offenses" (Rom 4:25). I confess that I don't understand the whole mystery about the death of Jesus on the cross. In speaking about the cross, the death of Christ, and our atonement, the New Testament writers use words like "ransom," "propitiation," "substitution," "deliverance," "representative," "reconciliation," "satisfaction," "sacrifice," and many others. But in some way or another, the biblical writers were trying to tell us that through the death of Jesus Christ, God did something for humanity that humanity could not do for itself. The biblical language contains something of the mystery, awe, and eternal sacrifice of such an act. No one theory can possibly explain what God did for us on the cross of his Son.

Years ago, when Germany was a more pastoral country, there was a man working high up on the steeple of a cathedral. One day he lost his footing, slipped, and fell from the scaffolding. There were sheep grazing below, and he fell on one of the lambs. The lamb perished, but the worker survived because the lamb broke his fall. When he returned to work, as a token of his gratitude, he carved the figure of a lamb in one of the stones over the entrance to the church.

In every church building, there ought to be an image of the lamb—the Lamb of God—who laid down his life for us. But it needs to be carved in our hearts, not merely in stone.

## The Slain Lamb

When Jesus was hanging on the cross, he cried, "It is finished" (John 19:30). The disciples certainly thought it was finished, didn't they? They thought their dream that the kingdom of God was going to become a reality was finished. They thought their hope that the new era of the Messiah was coming was finished. They thought their dreams and hopes were over and done with. But from the cross, Jesus cried with a loud voice, "*Telelestai!*" "It is finished," he said. "It is completed."

But what is finished? Jesus has finished bearing the sin of the world. He has finished identifying with humanity. He has finished his suffering. He has finished his redemption. He has finished his dying. He has finished restoring the bridge between humanity and God the Father. It is finished. And now you and I are called to accept, participate in, and share what Jesus has done for us.

Sometimes the Roman soldiers, who carried out the execution orders in the ancient times, would use a heavy mallet to break the legs of people hanging on crosses in an attempt to speed up their deaths. The Jewish leaders requested Pilate to carry out this act against Jesus. They smashed the legs of the thieves on both sides of Jesus. But when they came to him, they discovered that he was already dead. They did not have to break his legs (see 19:31-33). John then quotes from Psalm 34:20: "No bone of his shall be broken" (John 19:36). Then he quotes Zechariah 12:10: "They shall look upon him whom they have pierced" (John 19:37). Both of these are images of the Passover Lamb.

When they pierced Jesus' side with a spear, water and blood poured forth (19:34). Many interpretations have been given about the meaning of this water and blood. C. H. Dodd saw the flowing of blood and water from the side of Jesus as a "sign" of life that flows from the crucified and risen Lord.[3] This may be true, but I think it was simply John's way of conveying the medical understanding of the human body in that day. The human body was thought to be a balance of half water and half blood.[4] John was trying to make clear that Jesus had poured out his life. The witness—John the "beloved disciple"—said that Jesus had really died (see v. 35). There was no question about the death of Jesus. He didn't simply swoon. He was dead. The soldiers didn't even have to break his legs to make him die. They pierced his side to be certain he was dead. And dead he was. It was finished. His suffering and death were real.

In the middle of the stained-glass window behind the pulpit in my former church, St. Matthews Baptist Church in Louisville, Kentucky, a lamb is depicted in the middle. One Sunday, one of our members was sitting in church with her granddaughter. This small child looked at the lamb in the window and exclaimed, "It looks hurt." And it is. That image is symbolic of the Lamb of God who laid down his life for us.

## The Reigning Lamb

There is another picture of the Lamb in the Scriptures. In the book of Revelation, the word "lamb" is used twenty-nine times. The Lamb that was slain has now become sovereign; the Lamb that was victim has now become victor. This Lamb is a reigning, conquering figure. Twenty-nine times Jesus Christ is depicted as a conquering Lamb. The one who was slain is now victorious. He is the Lamb that saves the world from its sins. "Behold the Lamb of God that takes away the sin of the world."

Notice the first word John the Baptist uses in John 1:29: "Behold" (KJV). You have to behold the Lamb. You have to look at him. You have to do more than just hear sermons about the Lamb. You must behold him. You have to do more than simply hear hymns about the Lamb. You must behold him. You have to do more than merely look at paintings, drawings, or images of the Lamb. You have to do more than read about him. You must behold him. Let him come into your life.

All of us, because of sin, were a part of those who crucified Christ. We are all sinners and are aware of our fall at some point. Rembrandt, the seventeenth-century Dutch artist, painted a portrait of the crucifixion of Jesus called *The Raising of the Cross* (1633). In the painting one can see in the shadows behind the cross the faces of the people who helped crucify Christ. Among those faces in the shadows is Rembrandt's own face. He conveyed his involvement in his painting of Jesus' crucifixion.

We too were involved in the crucifixion of Christ. The answer to our sin is to look to the One who forgives us and redeems us. Behold the Lamb of God who takes away your sin and mine. Look to him!

Look to him and find redemption. Look to "the Lamb that was slain from the foundation of the world." As the hymn writer penned, "My faith looks up to thee, thou Lamb of Calvary, Savior divine! Now hear me while I pray, Take all my guilt away. O let me from this day be wholly Thine" (words by Ray Palmer).

## Notes

1. H. Wheeler Robinson, *The Cross in the Old Testament* (London: SCM Press, 1960), 192.

2. Quoted in Robert L. Short, *The Gospel According to Peanuts* (Richmond: John Knox Press, 1965), 36–37.

3. Quoted in George R. Beasley-Murray, *John* (Waco, TX: Word Books, 1987), 358.

4. Raymond E. Brown, *The Gospel According to John* XIII–XXI (Garden City, NY: Doubleday & Co., 1970), 947.

# Chapter 10

# The Supreme Sign: The Resurrection and the Life

## *John 11:17-57; 20:16-18*

The Gospel records indicate that Jesus often spent a great deal of time in the home of Mary, Martha, and Lazarus. Their home was located in a small hillside village called Bethany, which was about two miles from Jerusalem. Luke mentions an occasion in their home when Jesus engaged in conversation with the two sisters (Luke 10:38-42). John notes later in his Gospel that it was Mary who anointed the feet of Jesus (John 12:1-3). In the eleventh chapter of Mark, the Gospel writer states that Jesus often taught in Jerusalem during the day and spent the night in Bethany. That stay was most likely in this home. The Gospel writers also tell us that Jesus did not have a home, so his friends' house provided him with a comfortable place to spend the night, eat his meals, rest, and engage in conversation.

This family had listened to Jesus' teachings, shared meals together, and witnessed his mighty works. When Lazarus became gravely ill, it was only natural that they sent a messenger to Jesus with an urgent word. They assumed that Jesus would come immediately because of their friendship. They didn't think they had to ask him to come.

## Jesus Delayed

But for some reason Jesus delayed in coming to them. I am sure that the two sisters looked anxiously down the road toward Jericho, wondering why Jesus did not come. It most likely took the messenger a day to reach Jesus with the urgent message. Jesus then delayed two more days before he started toward Bethany. It would take Jesus a day's journey by foot to reach the town. By the time he arrived, four days had elapsed and Lazarus had died.

Why did Jesus delay? Some have suggested that he delayed so he could perform a miracle. But that is unlike Jesus. Jesus never performed a miracle for show. He resisted that temptation. In his Gospel, John always insists that Jesus' response was at his own initiative. When Jesus' mother urged him to take care of the problem of the shortage of wine at the wedding feast in Cana, Jesus told her in so many words, "I'll take care of it in my way" (John 2:3-11). When his brothers insisted that he perform his works in the public eye of Judea, Jesus informed them that "it is not yet time for me" (John 7:3-6). Whether it was mother, brothers, or friends, Jesus stated that the motive for his action came from his consciousness of God's plan for his life. "The Son can do nothing of himself, but what he sees the Father doing" (John 5:19). When Jesus did decide to make the trip to Bethany, his disciples reminded him of the danger awaiting him there from the religious authorities who had tried to stone him earlier. But after his short delay, he headed toward the home of his beloved friends.

## Lord, Where Were You?

We are told that Jesus loved this family. His delay was out of love, not lack of concern. When Jesus finally arrived, Martha, the more outspoken sister, met him. Martha seemed to be dependable, hardworking, and the one who was in charge of the family. Listen to her words when Jesus finally arrived: "Master, where were you? If you had been here earlier, we wouldn't be so sorrowful now" (John 11:21). But she also voiced a word of hope: "Anything you ask of God even now, I believe he will do it for you" (v. 22). She then went to her sister Mary, who was with the other mourners. Mary repeated almost the same words her sister said to Jesus but did not express much hope at this point (see v. 32).

"Lord, why did you delay?" We understand that question, don't we? Haven't there been times of illness or stress in your life or in the life of a friend when you have wondered why God seemed to delay in coming? You remember these moments well. You may have been sick. Your daughter was in an automobile accident and is now paralyzed. Your son was killed in the last war. You stand beside a loved one who is gravely ill in a hospital bed. You go weekly to a nursing home to visit a relative. Why does God linger elsewhere? Why isn't he here? Why doesn't he do something? "I have lost my job!" you exclaim. "I need help. Where is God? I cried to him for assistance, but there was no answer. Heaven seems to be made of brass. My call does not go through. I get a busy signal. God, where are you? Why do you linger?" We understand those questions, don't we? There are times when God does seem to delay his coming.

## A Sign to Glorify Christ

John the Evangelist has told us the purpose of this story from the start. He writes that the purpose of this sign is to glorify Christ. The word "glorify" in John's Gospel is a way of testifying about the cross, resurrection, and ascension of Christ (see John 12:23-26). The raising of Lazarus from the dead was to glorify Christ. It was a sign about Christ and his resurrection. John also notes that this sign—the raising of Lazarus—was the act that set the religious authorities in opposition to Jesus and led to his death.

"Lord, where were you?" Martha and Mary asked. Jesus responded to Martha, "Your brother will rise again." Almost as though she had heard the cliché, "It is the will of God," she responded to Jesus, "Oh, I know he will rise in the last day." At this moment Jesus gave his majestic affirmation: "*I am* the resurrection and the life. Whosoever believes in me, even if he dies, will live again. And anyone who is alive and believes in me shall never die" (John 11:25-26). What a statement! Then, right in the midst of her grief, Jesus asked Martha, "Do you believe this?" She responded with the highest statement of faith in the Gospels, one even greater than Peter's confession: "I believe that you are the Messiah, the Son of the living God, the One who was to come into the world" (v. 27). Her statement of faith came out of a personal awareness of the One who said, "I am." Her faith was not based on some abstract theological doctrine. She had personal acquaintance with the One who said, "*I am* the resurrection and the life."

## Life in the Present

Jesus spoke about the life that is *present*. This life is something that a believer can have in the present moment. But that concept can be hard for us to grasp. "I am the resurrection and the life," Jesus said. The life he offers is not sometime in the future in some other place; it's here, in the present. The word "life" is used more than thirty-three times in John's Gospel. "Life" is a larger word than "resurrection." Resurrection is part of the life of God. Life is something that is available to the believer today. John wrote, "This *is* eternal life, that they may know you, the only real God and Jesus Christ whom you have sent" (John 17:3). Resurrection life comes out of personal commitment to Christ as Lord. This is eternal life: to be in Christ.

On Easter morning when we speak once again about Jesus as the resurrection and the life, we are not merely pointing down the road to the time when you and I die. This resurrection life is a present possession now, something available in this moment. This is the life that Jesus Christ offers us today.

## Come Alive to Authentic Life

Lazarus symbolizes many things in this story. He represents more than a dead man in a grave. He also symbolizes those who are dead to authentic life. The poet Rilke wrote, "The deadliest death of all is to be alive and not know it." Many of us are not really alive. We have to admit that in fact we are dead to real life. Henry David Thoreau, on making a visit to New York City, observed, "I walked through New York yesterday—and met no real and living person."[1]

Many people go through life seemingly dead to it. The color of life has faded in their perspective. It is all gray.

These people stare without seeing, touch without feeling, taste without savoring, and hear without listening. They simply pass through life but remain detached and uninvolved. They have no sense of meaning or purpose in their living. They have come to a dead-end street filled with routineness and dullness. There is an absence of joy. Instead, they are filled with depression, sorrow, and anxiety. The word "anxiety" comes from a root word that means constriction of breathing. Too many of us feel constrained and tied up in knots. We are really not alive to life. We are dead to real life.

In one of Ingmar Bergman's movies titled *Wild Strawberries*, a professor dreams he is taking a walk one morning. As he rounds a corner, he comes upon a funeral procession with a horse-drawn wagon that is bearing a coffin into a churchyard for burial. Just as the wagon rounds the corner, the coffin falls off the wagon and lands in front of the professor. When it hits the ground, the lid comes open and the corpse falls out at his feet. Before he realizes what he is doing, he reaches down and tries to put the body back in the casket. As he does, the corpse grabs him and they struggle until they stand face to face. When he looks into the face of the dead man, he sees his own face. He wakes up from his dream and knows its meaning instantly: he had been living as a dead man. He has been living in the past. His thinking and attitude have been focused in the past. He is like a walking corpse.

Jesus says, "This is life." He calls to you and to me and asks us to come out of our deadness. But we don't want to acknowledge that we are living as dead people. Many of us are literally dead to life. Jesus calls to us to come forth from our graves and find life—the abundant life. When George Papashvily was a small boy in Caucasus, Russia, there was a tradition of young boys visiting a hermit and giving him a gift in exchange for a special proverb. George approached the old hermit with his gift in his trembling hands. After George told the hermit as best as he could about what he wanted to do in life, the hermit leaned over and whispered these words in his ear as his gift to the young lad: "This minute, too, is part of eternity."[2] George said that he was a much older man before he realized what that proverb meant.

This minute, this hour, this day is a gift from God, a part of eternity. Come out of your deadness. Find the resurrected life that Jesus Christ seeks to give you.

## The Deep Concern of Jesus

Notice the concern of our Lord as he stood before the tomb of Lazarus. John notes that the mourners were wailing. They were not just crying; they were shrieking. The ancient belief was that the louder one mourned, the greater their expression of grief. At this point, John says that Jesus groaned within himself. The Greek word for groan is really "to snort" like a horse. Why? This is a word expressing anger. Was Jesus angered by the superficial mourning, which had no real meaning to those who were doing it? Was he angered by the power of evil that the death of Lazarus symbolized? Was he groaning because of people's lack of understanding of who he was and the purpose of his ministry? We don't know.

## The Tears of Jesus

Standing before the tomb of Lazarus, John records two words that likely make up one of the first verses children memorize due to its brevity: "Jesus wept" (John 11:35). Why did Jesus weep? We are not sure. He wept obviously from grief for the family. But some have suggested that maybe Jesus grieved for what Lazarus would have to give up. The tears of Jesus were an indication of his own humanity. We do not worship a God who is unmoved by our concerns. The tears of Jesus indicate that God feels our pain, knows our sorrows, and understands our heartaches. Jesus wept.

# The Tomb of Lazarus

An ancient tomb was often located in a cave. A track was constructed in front of the cave to hold a large stone. The stone, which was sometimes the size of an oxcart wheel, was rolled across the track to close and seal the cave. Jesus said, "Remove the stone" (John 11:39). But Martha protested, "Lord, it has been four days! There will be an odor now. Lord, don't do that" (v. 39). Did she think that Jesus only wanted to satisfy his curiosity by looking on Lazarus's face again? Ancient Jewish people used to believe that the spirit lingered around the body for three days before it departed to Sheol. Was the reference to four days an affirmation that Lazarus was really dead? "Remove the stone," Jesus cried. Why didn't he remove it himself? If he had the power to raise a dead man, why couldn't he move the stone? Could this not show that God always wants our cooperation? We work with him. He doesn't move in opposition to us. We work together. "Remove the stone."

# Calling You Out of Your Tomb

Then, with a loud voice Jesus called into the tomb, "Lazarus, come forth" (John 11:43). As you are reading now about resurrection and life, reflect on the question, "What tomb are you buried in?"

Why are you living like a dead person? What tomb do you need to hear Jesus calling you to leave? Is it failure? Is it some secret sin, guilt, unbelief, doubt, lust, addiction to alcohol or drugs? What is your tomb? Let Jesus Christ free you from that tomb so you will not remain trapped. He is resurrection and life. He is one who can give you real purpose and meaning. Why stay buried in some tomb when he has come to set you free?

Reuel Howe tells about a friend of his who had terminal cancer. He visited his friend one day and was surprised at his courage and insight. On one occasion the friend told Howe,

> When I began to work through this experience, I made an amazing discovery. And it is this: "For every exit, there is an entrance." All the way through my life I have been having to give up things in order to get

things. I've had exits in order to get entrances. I had to give up something in order to go to school. I had to give up something in order to take a job. I had to give up single life in order to get married. All the way through my life, I've died a hundred deaths. I have had to die for something in order to get something new and better. For every exit, there is an entrance. And death is one more exit to that which is more.

The friend asked Dr. Howe to officiate his funeral service. When Dr. Howe walked into the funeral home after his friend died, he noticed a sign over the door near the casket. That one word summed up his conversation with his friend: "Exit."[3]

## An Entrance into Life

Yes, every exit is also an entrance. Come out of your tombs. Find the "exit." Let this day be an entrance for you into abundant life, which Jesus Christ as the living Lord gives you now. Hear his voice as his voice rung out to Lazarus centuries ago: "Come forth." Hear him speaking to you. Moses heard the voice of God in a burning bush. The young boy Samuel heard God's voice at Shiloh. Isaiah heard God in the temple at Jerusalem. Saul heard the voice of Christ on the Damascus Road. Augustine at Milan heard Christ saying, "Take up and read." Listen to his voice speaking within your heart.

When you have this life, you have the assurance that this is eternal life. Death is not the end. Lazarus did die physically. We will all die physically. But the life that Jesus Christ offers us is spiritual life. Physical death does not end that life. It is resurrection life. It is the life of hope. It is life that stretches from this world in abundant living into the eternal realm, which God has prepared. This is life, John says, to know the Son. Each of us can experience resurrection life as a present reality. Come out of your tomb and have the life that is everlasting.[4]

Each year in Jerusalem before Easter dawns, crowds of pilgrims gather in the Church of the Holy Sepulchre. This church is built in front of the cave that is believed to be the tomb of Jesus. At midnight the pilgrims light a sacred fire in the cave, and each pilgrim receives a candle that is lit from the fire. Then the pilgrims light the lanterns that they have brought and go out into the darkness of that night carrying the flame that was lit from the tomb of Jesus.

I pray that you will put down this book with your life lit by the living flame that comes from the One who is the resurrection and the life. When you have resurrected life, not even death will end it. Jesus said, "I am the resurrection and the life. Whosoever lives and believes in me shall never die."

## Notes

1. William E. Cain, *A Historical Guide to Henry David Thoreau* (London: Oxford University Press, 2000), 23.

2. George and Helen Papashvily, "What the Hermit Said," *Evening Star* (May 8, 1949): 2.

3. Story from John Claypool, cited in "Through the Open Door," sermon from First Presbyterian Martinsville, Virginia, April 13, 2008 (firstpresbyterianmartins-ville.org/documents/Through_the_Open_Door_4-13-08_sermon.pdf).

4. For further study on this theme, look at my book, *Journey to the Undiscovered Country: What's Beyond Death* (Gonzalez, FL: Energion Publications, 2012).

www.ingramcontent.com/pod-product-compliance
Lightning Source LLC
LaVergne TN
LVHW021521080426
835509LV00018B/2588